Holy Spirit Radicals

Pentecost, Acts and Changed Society

Arani Sen

malcolm down
PUBLISHING

First published 2018 by Malcolm Down Publishing Ltd.
www.malcolmdown.co.uk

British Library Cataloguing in Publication Data
A catalogue record for this book is available from the British Library.

ISBN 978-1-910786-92-5

Cover design by Esther Kotecha
Art direction by Sarah Grace

Printed in the UK

Acknowledgements

This book is dedicated to Sue, Sharon and Andy, for those early Greenbelts, when the seeds were first sown.

I am indebted to Dr Mike Thompson and Dr John Proctor, my erstwhile teachers at the Cambridge Theological Foundation, for their guidance, pointing me towards apt academic references. Also to Professor Loveday Alexander for keeping me up to date.

Thanks are due to the congregations and people of St Jude and St Paul's, Mildmay Park, Emmanuel, Southall and Christ Church, Upper Armley for all I have learned from you, and with gratitude for all that God has been able to do in those treasured places. Also, thanks to Dave Young for enabling the opportunity for study leave, and the Gladstone Library for providing me with an inspiring space to write.

I express my gratitude to all those who helped with case studies and the many interviews I needed to complete in order to put this book together. You are all an inspiration.

All names have been changed with regard to people, churches and projects.

I am extremely grateful to all who have helped with proofreading and editing: Jon Layley, Joanna Sarkar, my gifted administrator, for all her unswerving help with typing, editing and the miracle of being able to read my handwriting. Heartfelt thanks go to Lis Williams for her most thorough editing and comments. Thanks to Malcolm Down for his belief in this book and his enthusiastic support at the publishing stage. Finally, and most precious to me, my devoted wife, Alison, who has lived through the birth pains, childhood and adolescence of the writing process, for her co-ministry, her wonderful support, encouragement and proofreading.

'In this engaging and challenging book, Arani Sen leads us through his reading of Luke and Acts to show how the heart of God is longing for the renewal of all creation, and how this transformation is brought about through the work of the Holy Spirit. With helpful questions for reflection at the end of each chapter, we are invited to become part of God's work of transformation, in the name of Jesus Christ and in the power of the Holy Spirit.'

The Archbishop of York, Dr John Sentamu

'*Holy Spirit Radicals* is easy to read but difficult to live. Half way between a study of Acts and a missiology for cities, this will be right up your street if you care about cities, justice, race, marginalisation, mental illness, poverty, the power of the Holy Spirit, incarnational mission and the church of Jesus Christ. Arani Sen writes with wisdom, hands-on experience, scriptural insight, deep compassion and prophetic urgency. His vision of the Kingdom of God for twenty-first-century Britain is a compelling vision.'

Andy McCullough, author of Global Humility

'If the Holy Spirit who anointed Jesus in Luke 4 is the same Spirit poured out by Jesus on the day of Pentecost, then this anointing is for a vocation "to bring good news to the poor" and "let the oppressed go free". Charismatic encounter is as inextricably linked with action for justice as it is with healing and evangelism. In this insightful reflection on Acts, enriched and illustrated by his experience of urban ministry, Arani Sen puts back together dimensions of ministry in the Spirit which should never have been separated, and gives practical guidance for action. Warmly recommended for anyone concerned to see the Holy Spirit bring transformation to their community.'

Graham Cray, Honorary Assistant Bishop, Diocese of York

Commendations

'Creatively using the Acts of the Apostles as a framework, Arani writes powerfully from his working experience in urban communities to speak for and from churches in these areas, seeking support for them from the wider church. In so doing, he passionately weaves together his concern for justice with powerful stories of God's transforming work in individuals and communities.'

Andy Jolley, New Wine's Head of Urban Ministry, Archdeacon of Bradford

'In this compelling reading of the gospel as we see it lived out in the Book of Acts, Arani Sen shares his longstanding determination to bring the love of Christ into the multi-faceted contexts of contemporary urban society. This book demands our attention.'

Alison Morgan, Mathetes Trust, author of *The Wild Gospel* and *Following Jesus*

'Rooted in the "good news" of the Gospel and a personal journey, this is a practical handbook of deep Spirit-based inspiration and hope for social action in our urban times. As an antidote to individualism the Church can be a basis for rebuilding communities that leave nobody out.'

Rt Hon John Battle, Chair Leeds Diocesan Justice and Peace Commission

'Arani Sen's unique perspective shows us how, in our troubled world, the Holy Spirit can enfold our thinking, working and praying and bring us to a place where grace cascades. Chastened Liberals like me need to read this book as much as those who enjoy the manifest moving of the Spirit.'

Ann Morisy, Community Theologian, author of *Beyond the Good Samaritan* and *Journeying Out*

'This book is a plea for charismatic Christianity to recover its radical edge. Arani takes us back to the book of Acts and roots us in examples from the world of the underside and the dispossessed. The poor are always our teachers – and there is much to learn here.'

Pete Broadbent, Bishop of Willesden

Contents

Introduction

To answer the questions 'Why did I write this book?' and 'Who is this book for?' I will begin by telling you something of my own journey of faith, my spiritual influences and my passions.

I was born and raised in the north of England at a time when widespread multiculturalism was still a relatively new phenomenon. My parents came from Calcutta (now Kolkata) in India. They were proud to be Bengali, with its intellectual, cultural, liberal heritage, which was the hub of their identity; they were Hindu, high caste. Yet they lived most of their life in England, in many ways living a Western middle-class lifestyle, but in others retaining many cultural practices from India. This marked the start of my life journey.

I grew up in an almost entirely white context, in the 1960s and 70s. My father was a bit of a pioneer and became the first Indian GP in Yorkshire; he served in a mining village, but had considerable social status. This created something of a complexity at infant school, as I was the only Indian and one of very few middle-class children. This made me a stranger at school, by virtue of my colour (in the days well before racist taunts were outlawed) and because of my social class. This was compounded by the fact that in India children would mix only with their own class or caste, society being highly delineated, and that affected who I would socialise with. At the age of eight, I was moved to a nonconformist public school, thereby alienating me completely from my village context.

As a child, therefore, I grew up feeling different. For a start, I was a different colour from everyone else and this made me very noticeable. This is not an issue today, when I am proud to be British Asian, but as a child it was an issue to grapple with. At times, though certainly not predominantly, it led me to feel that I was a stranger in my home country. It was the only country I knew – when I visited India, aged five, ten and fifteen, it felt an alien country, socially, culturally and economically. Aged ten, in Calcutta, I was haunted by images of displacement and poverty I could see from every window – of shanty towns and scantily clad homeless children, while we stayed in relative comfort with servants tending to our every need. Such experiences were undoubtedly formative in my faith journey.

Each day, I would continue to cross religious boundaries. At my school, daily chapel was purely Christian, perhaps with some moral tales thrown in. We would sing hymns to praise God and hear Bible readings. The latter did not attract my attention; the Authorised Version was used and seemed distant from everyday life. Nevertheless, I gained a very good knowledge of Bible stories through RE lessons and Sunday school (to which my parents sent me – another sign of Hindu tolerance). I continued to believe in God, in a deity, but had no understanding of who Jesus was. If anything, I felt Christian as much as I felt Hindu, although I was excluded from the sacrament of Holy Communion.

Where I struggled with Hinduism was in the area of caste and rebirth, particularly the belief that there could be an 'outcaste', the Dalits, the ritually *untouchables*. By the time I was a teenager, I found that I could not incorporate a system whereby, in the words of the prophet Amos, the needy are trampled on and the poor are crushed. Somehow, I fathomed that at the heart of Hinduism there exists a sense that your life situation is your karma, a kind of fatalism, and that things cannot improve. Despite all Indian government initiatives, there seems to be an inherent reluctance to alleviate poverty and caste from India: 'The elites in India defend their position on religious grounds, claiming that a person's position on the social hierarchy is a direct reward for his merits in his past life.'[1] I became interested in Christianity because of Jesus' teachings on love for the poor and oppressed, and his teaching on loving our neighbour. A Christian hope, a hope of sight for the blind and freedom for the captive, identifies my faith to this day and is cardinal to my own ministry. It is marked by an understanding that God is a God of love, who interacts with humanity to the extent that he himself has suffered and died on the cross and therefore is fully involved in human suffering.

While at university, I became more interested in the Christian faith. Through meeting Christians, I became aware that they had an inner peace and joy, as well as a love for others that I had not experienced ever before. My own encounter with Jesus Christ was unashamedly evangelical. One night when I was an undergraduate, Jesus Christ met with me in a mysterious yet powerful way: I understood quite suddenly that Jesus had died for me and was the way to God; it was through the classic 'bridge' diagram that the Holy Spirit spoke to me. I fell on my knees and asked for forgiveness and new life. I felt a very powerful sense of the Holy Spirit. It was a joyous and life-transforming moment and the start of a wonderful journey of Christian discipleship and service. My faith journey was no longer a search for God, but God met me through his Son.

As I began to read my Bible avidly, now in a modern translation, I was very much struck by the strong doctrines of justice, of loving and caring for the poor, and Jesus' own example. I began to grapple with the theology of the kingdom of God, which Jesus inaugurated and commanded us to continue. It begins with the story of God interacting with humanity, through Jesus' incarnation into the world, in human time and history. It is the story of Jesus, both fully human and fully God, who moved on earth, suffered as we do, experienced human emotions, and yet who was able to perform miraculous signs of the kingdom – healing the sick, giving dignity to the poor, and ultimately defeating death through resurrection. His command to the disciples to 'proclaim the kingdom of God and to heal' (Luke 9:2) is equally applicable to Christians today who are called to work together in bringing God's kingdom *now* (not just looking forward to the kingdom to come and therefore not getting involved in the world). For this purpose Jesus has given his Holy Spirit as a sign that his ministry is active in the world today: 'But you will receive power when the Holy Spirit comes on you; and you will be my witnesses in Jerusalem, and in all Judea and Samaria, and to the ends of the earth' (Acts 1:8).

My new-found Christian faith led me to a desire to be incarnational in changing the world. In John 1:14 it says, 'The Word became flesh and made his dwelling among us.' Jesus immersed himself in a particular culture and context. For us, being 'incarnational' is following Jesus' example. I thought, and still do, that Christ alone can bring change to the brokenness of the world. I had a hopeful idealism. After university, not sure what to do, much to the horror of my parents, I decided I wanted to serve the poor. Perhaps I would go to India and teach there. In fact, through a number of life events, I went to work for an evangelical Anglican church in a very urban, multicultural context in the Midlands. At first it was culture shock: the grilled windows and cramped streets of Industrial Revolution housing, but by then without the industry. Very soon, I began to thrive in this context, and became very positive about all that God was doing and was able to do. I got involved in youth work. This was around the time of a Billy Graham campaign and many people were becoming Christians. I lived in the vicarage, and as I was the only staff member, I took on the many roles of 'church worker', including visiting, youth work and leading services. I was also trusted to preach, and found I had a gift for this. I began to sense a calling to ordained ministry, and a ministry very much in the inner city. Around this time, I first encountered the Holy Spirit powerfully.

When I first became a Christian, I did not have a strong understanding of the ministry of the Holy Spirit. I went to a classically 'evangelical' church, and was part of a university Christian Union, where the primary aim was to use every opportunity to share our faith, whether appropriate or not. With characteristic student zeal, I tried to convert anyone I could make contact with – conversion being a personal acceptance of Christ. At this time, there was something of a gulf between charismatics and those who were not; there was still quite a lot of suspicion on either side. In all honesty, I did find the charismatics rather daunting, with their hand-waving and unruly freedoms, as well as their unpredictable worship. I was much influenced by those who thought this was unbiblical. This was my view at the time.

The Holy Spirit had already begun to work in me, as I found myself becoming more open to the Spirit's work in my life. One evening, I went with a large group to a meeting to hear a well-known charismatic preacher. When the 'altar call' was given for those who wanted to be filled with the Spirit and speak in tongues, I was open to this. I went up for prayer but nothing happened, although I did feel an overwhelming sense of peace. However, a few days later while praying at home, I found myself speaking in tongues. This resulted in a greater freedom in worship, an openness to God's leading, the power of healing ministry and unveiling of my spiritual gifts.

Three strands came together in my life, and these remain my passions: encountering personal salvation, receiving a baptism of the Holy Spirit and a love of justice.

I spent time at the Greenbelt Festival, and here encountered many influential speakers speaking on themes of justice, peace, the poor and the oppressed. There was a biblical vision of a just world, the kingdom of heaven now, and we were God's partners in this. This was very stimulating, yet I remember thinking that the majority of charismatics in the churches were mainly teaching personal doctrines of conversion and being filled with the Holy Spirit. There was virtually no teaching on social justice in the evangelical church, and I did not know of many social projects in evangelical churches. Then the *Faith in the City* report came along, so the language changed, but I wonder if it impacted evangelicals that profoundly? I also wondered why so few evangelicals and charismatics were in the inner cities. I worked in an inner-city evangelical church and realised that it was the only church (out of twelve) in that tradition. I began to learn that in the nineteenth century, it was mainly the Anglo-Catholics who worked as the slum priests, serving the very poorest in society. There were a few exceptions, but in general, evangelicals had a passion to go out into the mission fields of the world to 'convert the heathen'. They did not often see the huge mission fields on their doorstep. This may still be the case, I fear.

The roots of this book go right back to my early Greenbelt festivals, when a book on a charismatic social theology began to germinate within me. My reading of the Bible has always reflected a strong practical care and compassion for the poor, the marginalised, and the outcast, as well as the power of God at work in his world though the Holy Spirit.

In the last thirty years, much has changed and many more evangelical and charismatic churches are involved in their communities, across denominations, and many run social projects. Yet, many churches and communities avoid the inner-city areas – and even more so, the outer estates. I set out to articulate a biblical vision of the early church, which desired to spread the message of Jesus Christ the Saviour, see people filled with the Holy Spirit, pray for and witness signs and wonders *and* see society transformed in terms of just practices and a compassion for the excluded and marginalised. Each chapter will begin with an analysis of the issues facing the church in Acts, in chapters 1–12, within the context of the early church growing rapidly and defining itself in a climate of fierce opposition and prejudice. Each chapter corresponds to a chapter in the book of Acts.

A very brief history of the charismatic movement

In Chapter 2 we will spend some time with the Azusa Street Revival, the juncture marking the birth of Pentecostalism. What characterises the Pentecostal Church is the theology of 'The Baptism in the Holy Spirit'. For Pentecostals, all Christians receive the Holy Spirit at the point of accepting Christ, but they believe in a separate post-conversion experience of a 'baptism in the Holy Spirit', resulting in the person speaking in tongues. Tongues, to the Pentecostals, is a heavenly language. Pentecostals look to the book of Acts where it says that on the day of Pentecost, disciples who had already made a decision to follow Jesus 'were filled with the Holy Spirit and began to speak in other tongues' (Acts 2:4). Another example is when Paul asked the Ephesians if they had received the Holy Spirit, after which 'the Holy Spirit came on them, and they spoke in tongues' (Acts 19:2–6). The Assemblies of God, a branch of Pentecostalism, declares in its Statement of Fundamental Truths: 'The baptism of believers in the Holy Ghost is witnessed by the initial sign of speaking with other tongues as the Spirit of God gives them utterance (Acts 2:4).' For Pentecostals, the phenomenon of speaking in tongues is seen as something all Christians should aspire to. It is usually manifested through the laying of hands on the Christian believer. There is generally great excitement when a Christian speaks in tongues.

By the 1960s, there was a new move of the Holy Spirit, moving across the established denominations in the UK and USA most notably – Anglicans, Baptists, Catholics and others were affected. Simultaneously, there emerged the 'House Church' movement which also looked to the model of the church in Acts, meeting in homes and not in church buildings. This was very new and radical and certainly had, and continues to have, a massive impact on Christianity in the UK and globally. (Nowadays many of the house churches have become more mainstream – Newfrontiers, Vineyard, Pioneer, to name a few – now often with very large congregations, meeting in warehouse-type buildings and not in homes, although the cell/house group structures are still important as 'house' meetings.) The house churches were characterised by the term 'Restorationism', restoring the church back to how (they interpreted) it was in the New Testament. In these churches, they emphasised extended free worship, raising hands and the supernatural signs of the kingdom being enacted. These include: tongues, healings, the spiritual gifts and prophecies. Emphasis was not on tongues alone but on all the spiritual gifts or *charisms* of the Holy Spirit, as expounded by Paul in 1 Corinthians 12–14. The kingdom of God was understood by the outpouring of God's Spirit on his church, empowering the church through signs and wonders, to draw others in – when someone experiences healing, it follows they seek the source of their healing, Jesus Christ, alive and powerful. There often was not a pastor as such, but a team of elders. Services were not formal and planned, the mantra was 'let the Spirit lead', as there was an openness to listening to the Holy Spirit. In these services there was often a sense of joy and excitement, and anticipation of God being at work.

In the traditional denominations, the charismatic movement became more widespread, also, from the 1960s. By the early 1980s it had seeped into much of the Anglican Church and the Baptist Church, although not without problems. There were a large number of church splits, often causing great pain to the church leaders – I knew of two church leaders who suffered heart attacks arising from the stress of such splits, instigated through a conflict between the 'charismatics' and those who were sceptical of the charismatic movement. Many clergy/ pastors who had been touched by the charismatic movement, and had received gifts of the Holy Spirit so powerfully, encountered hostility when trying to change their services. I have been to one church when the vicar (before my time) was so exasperated at the robed choir blocking the music group from doing anything that one night he burnt all their robes! Fortunately, now, in the twenty-first century, the charismatic movement is well accepted, and is not unusual in many evangelical churches.

The theological influences have included Dennis Bennett, David Pytches, David Watson and the Vineyard leader John Wimber. Wimber has been a profound influence on the charismatic movement, through his conferences in the UK in the 1980s and 90s. He propounded the importance of seeing 'signs and wonders' – for him, the reasons why churches did not experience signs and wonders were simply that these churches did not expect to see the miraculous. He asserted that we have been corrupted by the rationalism of the Enlightenment, and therefore expect all things to have a rational, scientific basis. A new way of thinking and behaving is required: the miracles, healings, signs and wonders require us to be expectant, and not to limit God. The influence of Wimber continues in the New Wine movement today, which has challenged many established churches to be hungrier for a God of miracles, of power and transformation. The New Wine movement and many of the former house churches seem to reach more people in the south-east or wealthier areas of the UK. It seems to be in the south and suburban areas of cities and towns where the biggest churches may be found, with a few exceptions. Many areas are not being reached with the life-changing gospel. Like the apostles, my prayer is that we may be rooted by the Spirit in order to leave behind our comfort zones and go to the areas where there is greatest human need. Indeed, there is need everywhere. Examine for yourself the community God has placed you in. Which groups are unreached? Where can you serve your community in practical ways, showing God's love in action? Throughout, we will look at case studies of ways churches have engaged in social action whilst not compromising their spiritual purpose.

One difference between Pentecostalism and the charismatic movement is the emphasis on tongues. Although this is a gift that is encouraged, to be 'filled with the Spirit' is more fundamental and can be an ongoing process. The gift of tongues may be sought, as the Alpha course, for example, overtly encourages, but it is not a compulsory sign of a Spirit-filled Christian.

I have found that the charismatic movement has brought great expectation into the church: a return to the standpoint of the apostles in the Acts of the Apostles, who expected God to move in power, bring people to faith in Jesus, and expected to see healings and lives transformed. There were physical manifestations of the Spirit at every turn. As I have already outlined, my understanding of the coming of the Spirit transcends the personal. In many charismatic churches, the emphasis is on 'me', on my needs, on my own experience of God; many of our songs are focused on 'I' as the subject – me and God. Indeed, I agree that we need this encounter with God, we need renewal, we desire healing and we are required to be more Christ-like. But for many charismatics, certainly historically, it stops here. The 'Toronto Blessing' of the 1990s was powerful, but people also may have sought a personal supernormal spiritual experience such as hysterical laughter as a form of personal release.

In the book of Acts, this personal experience of the Spirit would lead the person or group affected to the next stage of God's mission. Acts is a story not only of individual lives being touched by God, sins forgiven and being filled with the Holy Spirit. It is story of whole communities being changed, of the excluded included, of the barriers of prejudice and racism being broken down, of the poor and marginalised being cared for. Last but not least, it is about the church growing – a church for all people, regardless of background, race, ethnicity, social status or gender. This is what we will explore: the charismatic movement is not just about personal experiences, but if we really follow the injunction of Acts, it is about the Spirit permeating all areas of life and society, especially where there is need for transformation, social and personal.

This is not intended to be a commentary on Acts, but I will raise issues that I have found pertinent, as the early church carried together both a powerful move of the Holy Spirit and living out values that Jesus taught them. Luke shows a deeply rooted compassion for the poor in his gospel, and it is he who is chronicler of the story of the early church, so my starting point is to read Acts as a continuation of Luke's gospel. In each chapter we will then look at examples of how the life and transformation of the early church is being lived out today, with the challenges it faces in a very much still divided society. The testimonies and case studies are based on true examples of individuals but I have chosen to anonymise them, to protect the identity of the people concerned. I have changed the names of the church communities cited – they are based on real examples. The idea is for you to reflect on these and ask pertinent questions about what the Holy Spirit may be challenging you to do, in terms of justice, calling and serving your own communities.

I hope and pray that you will be challenged by the Holy Spirit as you read this, as well as be inspired. In many ways, this is a fresh reading of Acts, as I set out to marry together the coming of the Holy Spirit, the charismatic movement and the transformation of society.

At the end of each chapter, there is a short Action section, for you individually or in a group to grapple further with some of the questions and challenges, and further impetus for action in the book's conclusion.

Endnotes

1. V. Samuel, quoted in Chris Sugden, *Seeking the Asian Face of Jesus: The Practice and Theology of Christian Social Witness in Indonesia and India 1974–1996* (Oxford: Regnum, 1997).

1
Luke and the Kingdom of God

'Which of these three do you think was a neighbour to the man who fell into the hands of robbers?' The expert in the law replied, 'The one who had mercy on him.' Jesus told him, 'Go and do likewise.'

Luke 10:36–37

Luke scribed the most famous of parables, the Good Samaritan, which in many ways epitomises Luke's theology: Christian love must be sacrificial as well as practical; power structures are critiqued and the socially excluded are held up as examples. We are inclined to read Luke and Acts separately. For a start, in the canon, they do not follow on from one another – John is placed in-between. The way we read, write about and preach on both books is different – more is made of Luke's commitment to justice and the poor in his Gospel, as well as the miracles. In Acts 1–12, emphasis is centred on the power of the Holy Spirit and the growth of Christianity, but little is written about Luke's coverage of the poor and socially excluded in Acts.

There is a 'narrative unity' between Luke and Acts – Luke leads naturally on to Acts: 'Both the end of Luke and the beginning of Acts contain important statements in which Jesus commissions his representatives for their new task'.[1] In Luke 24, Jesus is forewarning the disciples that he will ascend back to Father and that this will be the last time he sees them: 'I am going to send you what my Father has promised; but stay in the city until you have been clothed with power from on high' (Luke 24:49). At the beginning of Acts 1, writing again to Theophilus, Luke comments that while with the disciples, Jesus ordered them not to leave Jerusalem but to wait there for the promise of the Father (v. 4). So the narrative unity is affirmed, and the scene is set for the Spirit to come. The disciples are reminded of John the

11

Baptist's promises, narrated in Luke 3:16 that he baptised with water, but they will be baptised with the Holy Spirit.

In this chapter, we will begin by trying to understand Luke. What are his passions and what themes underline his thinking? How does Luke's passion for justice and bias to the poor, as well his dependence on the transforming, healing power of the Holy Spirit flow into his narration of the Acts of the Apostles? We will begin by looking at some examples from Luke's gospel to see how he understands the kingdom of God, and throughout we will explore how this understanding permeates Luke's portrayal of the early church, as it emerges, in Acts.

What defines Luke?

Understanding what motivates Luke will help us to see that similar issues concern him in Acts as in his gospel. In Acts 1 the disciples pose this fundamental question to Jesus: 'Lord, are you at this time going to restore the kingdom to Israel?' Jesus' reply gives a strong indication of how Luke sees the kingdom of God, which throughout the book of Acts will spread from the people of Israel to the Samaritans, to the Gentiles, to the ends of the earth. What Jesus says to the disciples gives us a strong foretaste of what is to come:

> It is not for you to know the times or dates the Father has set by his own authority. But you . . . will be my witnesses in Jerusalem, and in all Judea and Samaria, and to the ends of the earth.
>
> Acts 1:7–8

Luke was probably a Gentile convert. In Colossians 4:10–14, Paul describes three of his co-workers as 'the only Jews among my fellow workers', and then mentions three further companions, including Luke 'the doctor'. We can infer from this that Luke is a Gentile. Perhaps his passion for the excluded, the Samaritans and the Gentiles ensued from his own experiences of feeling an outsider when apostles were mostly ethnically Jewish.

The context is first-century Palestine, the Palestine in which Jesus moved, healed and preached. It was a strongly hierarchical society: at the top, there was the royal court (e.g. Herod's court), which comprised the very affluent, as well as politically powerful. Herod may have owned up to half the land in the dominion. The land-owning classes also hired tenants, very much the poor, who were at the mercy of the landowners. The second class were the wealthy: the merchants and landowners, but also the religiously powerful. There is evidence of four high priestly families, who profited from the Temple (sacrifices, Temple tax, the sale of Temple animals, the profits of moneychangers). There was also a class of skilled artisans; Jesus' earthly father, Joseph, as a carpenter, would fit into this bracket.[2]

Finally, there are the poor. The poor were a very sizeable proportion of the total population and therefore highly significant. The lowest of the low were the beggars, e.g. in the Temple (Acts 3:2–3), and the sick and possessed. In Luke's gospel, the mention of 'crowds' in various crowd scenes probably relates to the poor, including the sick and demon-possessed. This is seen in Luke 7:21–22 and also in Luke 6:18–19, when Jesus' power is depicted as so great that the whole crowd was healed.

Poverty is shown to be anathema and scandalous in God's eyes. This whole understanding of Luke's emphasis flows into my reading of Acts. Peter summarises Jesus' ministry as being anointed by the Holy Spirit to fulfil God's purposes:

> You know what has happened throughout the province of Judea . . . how God anointed Jesus of Nazareth with the Holy Spirit and power, and how he went around doing good and healing all who were under the power of the devil, because God was with him.
>
> Acts 10:37–38

It is the Holy Spirit who has anointed Jesus for his mission at the very beginning of his ministry; he comes as the fulfilment of Old Testament hopes. Drawing on Isaiah 61:1–2, Jesus proclaims:

The Spirit of the Lord is on me
because he has anointed me
to proclaim good news to the poor.
He has sent me to proclaim freedom to the prisoners
and recovery of sight to the blind,
to set the oppressed free,
to proclaim the year of the Lord's favour.

Luke 4:18–19

As with the Old Testament prophets, it is the Spirit who anoints Jesus' mission to the poor, the captive, the blind and the oppressed. The word 'today' (v. 21) is also important: 'Today this scripture is fulfilled in your hearing'; Jesus' message receives meaning in the context of Jesus' lifetime. It is *now* that Jesus is proclaiming liberty to the poor and oppressed; it is they who will be restored to the Lord's favour.

References to the Jubilee are also found in this context.[3] Reflecting the language of the Jubilee, Jesus will engage in acts of justice to debtors, the homeless, the impoverished and the marginalised. This call also fits in with Luke's concept of the kingdom of God, where social justice is to be an attainable goal in the present age. In the 'Sermon on the Plain', it is the literal poor who are blessed, 'for yours is the kingdom of God'. The poor in Luke's beatitudes are those on the margin, the excluded and reviled; Luke concerns himself with the stark realities of poverty. Luke gives hope to the poor, it is they who seem to inherit the kingdom, and it is they who will laugh when the kingdom comes (Luke 6:20–23).

There is so much emphasis on the renunciation of property as a sign of discipleship. Dr Luke is educated and presumably wealthy, yet following his conversion, he emphasises renouncing worldly wealth, and clearly wants Theophilus, and his readers, to grasp this too. In Luke, the disciples leave everything when they follow Jesus (Luke 5:11); Levi does the same (Luke 5:27–28). Those who have possessions are called to share these and give them away (e.g. Luke 6:30) – very much the values of Acts. Today we can translate this as generosity. Can we be radically generous in our love and care for the poor and excluded, whilst reaching out with Jesus' message of repentance and liberty from our past, as we embrace Jesus' offer of new life?

Anointed for mission: the beginning of the Acts of the Apostles

There is an equally important aspect to the work of the Holy Spirit in Luke. This is the power of the Holy Spirit to intervene in this world to bring in God's healing, God's transformation and God's grace. This forms the basis of the 'kingdom theology' much quoted in charismatic circles. For me, this is an essential aspect of the work of the Holy Spirit but, as I have argued above, it is not the whole picture. Practical love, care and transformation of the situation of the materially poor is not an add-on, but an essential part of Christian calling.

In Luke 9, Jesus gave the disciples a foretaste of building his kingdom in the power of his Spirit: 'When Jesus had called the Twelve together, he gave them power and authority to drive out all demons and to cure diseases, and he sent them out to proclaim the kingdom of God and to heal those who were ill' (vv. 1–2).

At this stage, it is the twelve disciples, but soon he calls the seventy-two (Luke 10:1–24) and sends them out. To be a disciple means to be willing to be trained for and sent out on a mission. Jesus taught his disciples by gathering them together, teaching them and then sending them out. Being 'sent out' is a crucial theme in Acts. The word 'mission' comes from the Latin *missio*, 'I send'.

Once he has called them together, he gives them power and authority. This is supernatural power; the Greek *dunamis* captures the actual sense of the power needed to perform the miraculous. The other word in Greek is *exousia*, and refers to God-given authority. Jesus first gives them power and authority, then the commission to preach and heal. To begin with, the disciples see Jesus exercise miraculous power over demons. Next, they share in his power and authority when one of the Twelve confronts a demon on their mission. The disciples are also given both the ability and the authority to heal. Finally, the disciples are given a mission to preach, but they are not just commissioned as orators, they are to proclaim the kingdom of God as ambassadors. The content of their message is 'the kingdom of God'. This is a foretaste of what is yet to come when the Holy Spirit comes on them in full.

In Acts 1, the disciples and the women, including Mary, Jesus' mother, are preparing to be anointed for mission. Luke is inclusive in his approach and the women are equal partners in God's mission. Jesus puts the gathered assembly in the picture: 'You will receive power when the Holy Spirit comes on you; and you will be my witnesses in Jerusalem, and in all Judea and Samaria, and to the ends of the earth' (Acts 1:8). Now the context is set for Acts 1–9: the Spirit will lead the disciples from Jerusalem, as their base, reaching the Jewish people with the call to Jesus' transforming power, subsequently the Samaritans, and finally the ends of the earth – mission to the Gentiles. This new-found spiritual energy and mission is no longer for the chosen few – interestingly through Acts we will see how the Jewish people were the least responsive, the ones most caught out by tradition, laws and regulations, and the ones most unlikely to freely accept God's grace. The Samaritans symbolise the outcasts who are close to Luke's heart. In the Jewish culture, ridden with purity laws, it would be unthinkable for a Jew such as Jesus to ask for water from a Samaritan.[4] Jesus pre-empts what will happen when the Spirit comes – to him, there are no outsiders, no excluded, no marginalised groups. The Holy Spirit is for everyone and is part of the process of finding salvation, through Jesus Christ. As Peter tells the crowd at Pentecost:

> Repent and be baptised, *every one* of you, in the name of Jesus Christ for the forgiveness of your sins. And you will receive the gift of the Holy Spirit. The promise is for you and your children and for all who are far off – for all whom the Lord our God will call.
>
> Acts 2:38–39 (emphasis mine)

Access is free and it is unencumbered by culture, prejudice, race, class or gender.

The importance of Jerusalem

Just before the dramatic moment of his ascension back to heaven, Jesus commands the disciples not to leave Jerusalem but to wait there for the 'gift my Father promised'. It is highly unlikely that they would have any real idea what form this gift would take.

It is the implication of Jerusalem as the location for these extraordinary events that I want to explore. God has a heart for the city. In Luke 9:51, Jesus sets out for Jerusalem. Tannehill finds here further narrative unity between Luke and Acts – Jesus is setting out for Jerusalem as a precursor for the next stage of ministry, following his death. Jerusalem will be the place where Jesus is tried and executed, but following his resurrection it will be in Jerusalem that the Holy Spirit will be poured out and the church will be born in great power.[5]

Jerusalem was an important urban centre, and the significance of an urban, multicultural city as the place from which the message about Jesus Christ will be proclaimed is central to what happens in Acts. Cities, like Jerusalem, were and still are characterised by high-density populations. Ancient cities like Jerusalem were surrounded by walls, to give them a sense of security and containment. In Psalm 122 David prays: 'May there be peace within your walls and security within your citadels.' Jesus himself was treated as an outsider, by being crucified outside the walls – the place of criminals, of disputes, of unwholesome activities, of bloodshed. It is in cities that we find palaces, political institutions and courts. In short, cities are political and judicial centres.

Cities are also places where 'outsiders' can flock to and find refuge: they are places where immigrants can come; where the excluded can come and hide. For example, in India, in cities the population can exceed 10 million because people flock there from rural areas hoping to build a better economic future. In India, those persecuted by caste in rural settings can easily find a fresh new identity in the city and build a new life for themselves, as well as economic migrants and street children (also escaping their context). In Delhi, I met ten- and eleven-year-old boys who had been street children, now looked after in a Christian-run home. Some had run away from abuse; some were simply forced to leave because the family could not afford to feed them. Once in Delhi they became victims of gang lords who had a hold on them, forcing them to beg or collect scrap – in effect a form of slavery. The Christian project I visited, in a slum, served to rescue street children from this underworld, feed, educate them and help them train for a trade.

Cities are also places of economic and business activity, and in the developing world it is to the cities that people come looking for work. For example, in South Africa in 1990, just before the collapse of apartheid, there was a 75 per cent growth of population in the city of Durban and most lived in shanty towns. People flocked and still flock to cities to find hope, to find work, to find a future. In this scenario crime flourishes, on an economic level, as it is almost impossible to police illegal employment and the black market. Crime burgeons through gangs, through drug dealing, through antisocial behaviour (often a response to a sense of hopelessness). It is to cities that migrants flock, in biblical times and now. So, in Jerusalem on the day of Pentecost, a list of fifteen different nationalities and ethnicities is given. A mixture of inhabitants and visitors, people on business, were all touched by the Holy Spirit. Jerusalem was a highly multicultural, multi-faith city – some of those touched by the Spirit were not devout Jews, but people of other faiths.

Cities are also noted for great social inequalities – this will become clearer as you read on, and this is an issue that has remained constant in the history of human civilisation.

In the first century AD, as in the world today, the majority lived in cities. When we think of cities, what do we think of? Perhaps we conjure up a city break – sightseeing the fine, historic architecture; sampling the many trendy bars and restaurants, the high-vis. department stores. But what is behind the façade? Prague is smart and stylish in the centre, but if you travel in on the train, you see block after block of monochrome, concrete, high-density ex-communist blocks of flats.

What image does 'inner city' conjure up for you? Stereotypically they are places to be avoided: places of crime, of drug dealers, of betting shops and street drinking. My wife and I have a particular love for and a calling to the 'inner city'. We find them places of great vitality, fuelled by such a wonderful diversity of people, of needs, of joys, of pain, of hope. In inner cities, wealthy and poor live in close proximity; different cultures live as neighbours. In churches, hopefully, people look out for one another, try to get involved in their community, use their resources and buildings for the community as a whole, and are being incarnational. Of course, inner cities can be complex and difficult places too. I read a job description for an inner-city church leader that included the words, 'In the area there are considerably higher than average incidences of single-parent families, drug abuse, mental illness, crime and domestic violence.' I felt called, and took the job. It was very rewarding ministry.

If God has a heart for the city, shouldn't we too? The reasons are debateable as to why so few people feel called to minister or worship in inner cities. In an inner London borough where I served, it was common to meet residents of the inner city who worshipped in the large city-centre churches. I pray that people will see a vision for God's work in the inner city, and outer estates which are harder still, with their joys and struggles, but spiritually fulfilling, mind expanding, enriching ministries. Our joy has been to see asylum seekers who have fled persecution worshipping together with elderly white people, highly educated people, and those with learning difficulties and disabilities, and single parents – a whole cross-section of society. It is a joyful experience, and to me a reflection of heaven.

The context of Pentecost was in a milieu of social and cultural diversity and this is not underplayed in any way by Luke. In fact, much of what happened in Acts took place in cities. Following the work of the Spirit in Jerusalem, which remained the apostles' 'home base', Paul went with the message of Jesus to the great cities of the day on his missionary journeys – Ephesus, Athens, Corinth, Rome, to mention a few. It is from the cities that God's purposes can be fulfilled: an abundance of nationalities converge in cities, many hear the gospel, and then have influence on their families and friends. Cities are vibrant, dynamic places – Paul recognised this when he planted churches.

Ready and waiting

We are left with a sense of anticipation as Jesus' followers wait. I am sure they do not know the enormous impact the coming of the Holy Spirit will have on them and the people around them. They wait in Jerusalem, the city where Jesus left them – firstly through the terrible pain of the crucifixion, and now with his ascension into heaven, the last time they will see him after his resurrection. It is into this city that the Holy Spirit will erupt with earth-shaking, dramatic power. It is a city where, like our cities today, many races, nationalities, social groupings, social classes, different needs – a whole microcosm of God's world – come together. The Holy Spirit will impact every people, race, nationality and culture. The Holy Spirit will break down every preconception, every prejudice, every form of egotism and idolatry. The kingdom of God is here.

Action

- I have invited you to re-evaluate the relationship between Luke and Acts – not just in terms of structure but also the theological themes. Read Luke 24 and Acts 1 in one sitting – what do you notice?
- Reflect on Luke's heart for the poor, for example read the Mary's song, Luke 1:46–56 and Jesus' mission statement in Luke 4:14–21.
- What is your response to reading that the poor, the marginalised and the outcasts are very much part of God's redeeming work in Luke's gospel and Acts? What does this mean today?
- You may like to find out more about ministry in the inner city. Link up with a church in the inner city and find out the joys and challenges of this ministry.

Endnotes

1. R.C. Tannehill, *The Narrative Unity of Luke–Acts: A Literary Interpretation* (Minneapolis, MN: Fortress Press, 1990), p. 11.

2. Walter E. Pilgrim, *Good News to the Poor: Wealth and Poverty in Luke–Acts* (Minneapolis, MN: Augsburg, 1981), p. 31.
3. References to the Jubilee in the Old Testament refer to the seventh year when the harvest is to be donated to the poor, not kept for profit; slaves are to be set free; food shared, debts absolved, e.g. Exodus 21:2–6, Leviticus 25.
4. See John 4.
5. Tannehill, *Narrative Unity,* p. 11.

2
The Politics of Pentecost

Now what belongs together grows together.

Willy Brandt[1]

Willy Brandt uttered these words at the fall of the Berlin Wall in 1989. Brandt had served as West German Chancellor between 1969 and 1974, navigating through the Cold War and walking a tightrope in his relations with East Berlin. His heartfelt statement captured the emotional release of a new Germany, a new era of hope and new chances; a country once again united, allowing free movement and liberty between East and West. I myself lived in Berlin, as an eighteen-year-old gap-year student; this was a Berlin where the wall was visible everywhere, with its human traps, lethal dogs, barbed wire and guards with guns traversing the city and surrounding its perimeters. Reunification marked the end of this very inhuman and unnatural division through this great city. Berlin is once again a great 'world city', a symbol of a new country born out of its ashes.

The re-unification of all God's people is a key theme in Acts 2. Commentators often observe that Pentecost is an inversion of Babel. After the construction of the Tower of Babel: 'The miracle of languages reminds us of the scattering of Babel and God's promise that he would one day "change the speech of the peoples to a pure speech".'[2] The quote refers to Zephaniah 3:9, a post-exilic prophecy indicating the future restoration of Israel. At Babel (Genesis 11), the story is of the human, created in God's image, who depended only on their own power, and sought to play God. The summary is in the words, 'Let us build ourselves a city, with a tower that reaches to the heavens, so that we may make a name for ourselves'; they wanted to operate in their own power and achievement, seeking omnipotence, which can only belong to God. What ensued was that God scattered them abroad, confused their language and stifled their comprehension. All human language and communication became confused, the destructive power of the human mind was dissipated, so dependence on God was sought anew.

Unity at Pentecost

At Pentecost, Acts 2 testifies that all power comes from the Holy Spirit alone. All that takes place has nothing to do with any human behaviour or communication. Pentecost erupts, the Spirit wills it and the people respond. It is sudden and earth-shattering – a veritable colourful festival of movement, colour, fire, wind and light (vv. 1–3). Here were people gathered in Jerusalem for the Jewish festival of Shavuot (Pentecost) – many staying from Passover until Pentecost. Suddenly, in contrast to Babel, they are able to understand each other even though their mother tongues are diverse. At Pentecost the gospel was preached and accessible to every language represented, there was no predominant culture or superior race. The Holy Spirit broke down all barriers of language, race and nationality, pointing people to Jesus Christ alone, as Paul comments: 'For [Christ] himself is our peace, [it is he] who has made the two groups one and has destroyed the barrier, the dividing wall of hostility' (Ephesians 2:14). At Pentecost, the identity of Christians is as followers of Christ, not by their ethnicity, colour, race, gender or language.

In many cities, different languages are heard all the time. I travel into Leeds on the bus and hear Farsi, Arabic, Urdu and English – it is a wonderful, diverse sound, but I can only understand English and the odd Urdu word which I recognise from my scant knowledge of Bengali. In Jerusalem, the different cultures did not expect to understand each other's languages – no doubt they communicated in basic Aramaic or Greek. Suddenly each person could hear Galileans speaking every single native language – everyone could hear their own language and words about 'the wonders of God'. Gathered were 'Parthians, Medes and Elamites; residents of Mesopotamia, Judea and Cappadocia, Pontus and Asia, Phrygia and Pamphylia, Egypt and the parts of Libya near Cyrene; visitors from Rome (both Jews and converts to Judaism); Cretans and Arabs – we hear them declaring the wonders of God in our own tongues' (Acts 2:9–11). A truly diverse collection of people.

It must have been quite an event! Even then, there were some cynics who thought they were all drunk from too much all-night partying. The dominion of God breaks into human history, and the coming of the Spirit at Pentecost is seen as a means by which this age can be properly proclaimed and inaugurated as the age of salvation for all peoples, as 'a light for revelation to the Gentiles, and the glory of your people Israel' (Luke 2:32). At the heart of Pentecost is unity – God united people for the work that was to come. Cultural barriers and linguistic problems were all broken down. It is God who communicated, in the power of the Spirit. A new age was born. Signs of God's kingdom were the miraculous, and signs and wonders; the earth was literally shaking. Barriers of ethnicity were being broken down.

The earth-shaking events became the initiation of mission, from a tiny number of Jerusalem apostles to the ends of the earth, a mission 'reaching out beyond its small base in the church to all Jews and the Gentile world'.[3] The audience, trying to make sense of the events, received a scriptural exposition from Peter. All were called to repentance – Peter cited the prophet Joel which would have been familiar to his hearers. What Joel prophesied had now come to be true: the Spirit had been poured out on all flesh. Women and men were included: 'Even on my servants, both men and women, I will pour out my Spirit in those days' (Acts 2:18); this was very radical, as women in contemporary Judaism were very much secondary citizens. Servants in first-century society were literally property, dehumanised and without any rights. They too be will part of God's wonderful vision; they too will be renewed, set free, at least in a spiritual sense, and filled with the Holy Spirit.

Pentecost began with an open invitation – to anyone and everyone; then 'everyone who calls on the name of the Lord will be saved' (Acts 2:21).

The dominion of God breaks into human history, and the coming of the Spirit at Pentecost is the means by which this age can be properly proclaimed and inaugurated as the age of salvation for all peoples as a 'light for the revelation to the Gentiles and for the glory of your people Israel'.[4]

For Luke, Simeon's words in Luke 2 have been fulfilled – salvation is for everyone, it is a free gift. It is no longer the exclusive preserve of a chosen nation. Through Acts we will see this being fulfilled – the Jews first, then the Samaritans, then last, but not least, the Gentiles. Through the conversion of Saul, this will fire up the great missionary journeys, to spread news of Jesus 'to the ends of the earth' (Acts 1:8).

The revolution of Pentecost erupted – it turned upside down all accepted social and hierarchical structures. At its heart a message of welcome, of salvation, of transformed lives, of a call to be part of God's upside down kingdom. Tannehill discerns a pattern in Acts: the apostles were filled by the Holy Spirit; they then spoke God's word, performing signs and wonders, stimulating a response of acceptance or rejection.[5] Peter did not hesitate to accentuate that certain Jews were responsible for Jesus' death, and repentance was called for. We note too that the drama that is played out is Trinitarian in nature:

God is declared to be the hidden actor behind each stage of Jesus' story: his mighty acts (2:22), his death (2:23), his resurrection (2:24–32); his exaltation and the pouring out of the Spirit (2:33–34), his appointment as Lord and Messiah. God 'exalted' (2:33–35; 5:31) and glorified (3:13). The reversal is also implied in the repeated statements that 'you killed him but God raised him up.[6]

The resurrection of Jesus was the unprecedented miracle that then led to the outpouring of the Holy Spirit.

The birth of Pentecostalism

The birth of 'Pentecostalism' can be traced back to a revival in Azusa

Street, Los Angeles, in 1906. This powerful and transformational event can be seen as the genesis of the now worldwide Pentecostal and charismatic church. The reverend William J. Seymour, an African-American, designated the term 'baptism in the Spirit' even before he had experienced it. In 1906 he speaks of the 'divine call' that brought him from Houston, Texas, where he had been in theological training, to Azusa Street Mission, in Los Angeles. This was no ordinary theological training – no dry exegeses of Greek texts, or homiletics. Rather, the leader of the Bible school, Charles Parham, believed inherently that missionaries should be able to preach 'in the language of the natives'.[7] By 'language of the natives', Parham was referring back to Acts 2, when all could hear what was spoken about Jesus in their own tongue. He believed this phenomenon was not just for the first century after Christ, but of utmost contemporary importance.

The centrality of their mission was 'that we may go before the world with something that was indisputable, because it tallied with the Word'. The students were sent to research Acts 2, and they all concurred that in Acts 2 'other tongues' were spoken at the point of the 'Pentecostal blessing'. Well, it was not a case of, 'Well done students, go back to your studies' but instead, there was a watch-night service. During the service, sister Agnes N. Ozman asked for hands to be laid upon her to receive the Holy Spirit, as she felt called to 'foreign fields'. At first Parham had refused, as he had not received 'the experience' himself. However, he was persuaded, and nothing short of a miracle followed:

I laid my hand upon her head and prayed. I had scarcely repeated three dozen sentences when a glory fell upon her, a halo seemed to surround her head and face, and she began to speak in the Chinese language, and was unable to speak English for three days. When she tried to write in English to tell us what had happened, she wrote in Chinese, copies of which we still have in newspapers printed at that time.[8]

For my first degree, I studied French and German – it took me eleven years of hard slog, declining irregular verbs, understanding the future perfect, imperfect subjunctive and lots more to become fluent, so that was an incredible miracle – instant Chinese! More prayer, and more miracles took place after this event for Parham; he himself received the gift of tongues – in Swedish! There is something about the church at the very beginning of the twentieth century, having a sense of globalism, of being sent out to all the nations, and recovering the excitement of the first Pentecost. These events have shaped the whole charismatic movement in the world today. As we will see, it is a movement that today is particularly strong in Latin America and much of Africa. The church moved out of its closeted enclaves, to be a global, nondenominational movement, characterised by the Holy Spirit.

Azusa Street – the revival

Let us return now to Azusa Street in 1906. William Seymour had been 'educated' by Parham, had been opened up to the power of the Spirit, and had formulated a doctrine of 'the baptism of the Holy Ghost'. In his own words, 'for when the disciples were all filled with the Holy Ghost, they spoke in tongues as the Holy Spirit gave them utterance'.[9] Seymour then received the 'baptism of the Holy Ghost' – no doubt speaking in tongues, but in what form we do not know – was this a heavenly language or a language of the world, as with Parham's students? I am inclined to think this was spiritual phenomenon and a spiritual language.

Fired up by the Holy Spirit, and now believing strongly and preaching in the baptism of the Holy Spirit, Seymour was called by God quite definitely to Los Angeles, from Houston, Texas.

On 19 April 1906, Frank Bartleman describes what he experienced:

While sitting in the noon meeting at Peniel Hall, 227 South Main Street, the floor suddenly began to move with us. A most ugly sensation ran through the room. We sat in awe. Many people ran into the street, looking up anxiously at the buildings, fearing they were about to fall.[10]

He then felt called to go to Azusa Street, to a former old-frame (probably tin) Methodist building. Here, there was a multicultural gathering: 'we finally reached Azusa and there were about a dozen saints, some white, some colored. Brother Seymour was there in charge . . . the fire could not be smothered.'[11]

Over half a century before the Civil Rights Movement, and Martin Luther King, we are provided with a breathtaking and beautiful vision of black and white, of all races being united by the common denominator of the Holy Spirit. Here is a vision of a multicultural and classless church – a vision we may have lost again. However, the first Pentecostal church was socially transformational. It also seemed to be highly interdenominational, breaking down barriers – gradually, perhaps sadly, a new denomination was being born. Yet, the Pentecostal movement, which led to the charismatic movement, reached many of the denominations of the world.

Bartleman continues to accentuate both the spiritual and social transformation – at the birth of the modern-day charismatic movement, the two aspects go hand in hand. Both are part of who God is. He continues to write about social strata being challenged in the kingdom of God, 'All classes began to flock to the meetings . . . the rich and educated were the same as the poor and ignorant and found a much harder death to die. We only recognised God. All were equal.'[12] This is a radical vision of the kingdom of God, at a time when Western society was divided into their 'rich man in his castle, the poor man at his gate.'[13] When you visit historic churches, with huge box pews for the rich and barely a shelf for the servants, we see this is very ahead of its time. Everything rests on a supernatural understanding of who God is, a sense of the Holy Spirit transforming the individual life, creating holiness, and changing the focus from self to the kingdom of God. The Azusa Street people were lost in 'wonder, love, and praise'[14] and this enabled them to be lifted out of the trite, the destructive and dehumanising aspects of human behaviour.

This becomes clearer still when Bartleman writes about race:

> The 'color line' was washed away in the blood . . . they would not even allow an unkind word said against their opposers or the churches [the Press had vilified them]. The message was the love of God. It was a sort of 'first love' of the early church returned. The 'baptism' as we received it in the beginning did not allow us to think, speak or hear evil of any man.[15]

The Holy Spirit has brought love and transformation. As Paul wrote, on the much-quoted axis between his two chapters on the spiritual gifts (1 Corinthians 13), without love we are nothing. Contrast this with human nature, where it is symptomatic to be territorial or, at its worst, racist or classist.

The Holy Spirit creates a radical community

In Acts 2:37–42, the first converts are described. They had experienced the Holy Spirit. They did not comprehend what was going on at first, but Peter explained to them what had happened, and how this fitted in with what was foretold in the Old Testament. The message at this stage was directed to the Jews – 'Therefore let all Israel be assured of this: God has made this Jesus, whom you crucified, both Lord and Messiah' (Acts 2:36). Peter was proclaiming that the reign of God was here, that the promised Messiah is Jesus. The new converts were called to repent and be baptised in the name of Jesus, at which point they would receive the Holy Spirit. They were then exhorted to save themselves 'from this corrupt generation' (Acts 2:40).

About 3,000 people were added and presumably baptised – how the logistics of this worked I cannot fathom, with my organised, planned Western ways of thinking. But the miracle is that about 3,000 people were added to those who followed Jesus. Nowadays, we often invite people to an Alpha course, they come, and may be born anew. However, we often do not follow through with discipleship. The model in Acts is this: they devoted themselves to the apostles' teaching; they spent time together in fellowship, which included eating together, worship and sharing; they broke bread – Holy Communion as we know it, which was as natural as eating a bowl of bran flakes – it was not an elaborate ritual, but took place in the context of eating together; and last but not least, in prayer. They were immersed in worship, in its widest sense. Miracles happened, they were to be expected, and were a normal part of the new Christians' lives. These increased their faith – Luke speaks of their 'awe' – through seeing, learning about and experiencing God's power at work.

The next event is perhaps one of the most challenging, overlooked and ignored passages in the Bible: 'All the believers were together and had everything in common. They sold property and possessions to give to anyone who had need' (vv. 44–45). Acts 2:42–47, is a summary of their life in community. Luke emphasises how important this is by writing in a second summary of life in community (4:32–37). Tannehill explains:

> As the second summary of community life follows a renewed outpouring of the Spirit, there may be a suggestion that the Spirit not only inspires bold preaching and wonders (4:29–31) but also devotion to others and their needs (4:32).[16]

Tannehill also links these passages to Jesus' teaching in Luke 18:18–23, where Jesus exhorted the rich young ruler to sell all his possessions so that he can inherit the kingdom of God. Once again, we discover Luke's emphasis on caring for the poor and needy, and for the rich to be challenged in their worship of possessions. The result of this freeing up of individuals from idolising wealth, coupled with deeply focused worship, prayer and sharing is that the church grew miraculously.

It is no coincidence that the church today is growing fastest in China, Latin America and Africa, particularly in its charismatic and Pentecostal forms of worship. In many examples, inhabitants are beset by poverty, yet respond to Jesus Christ. With the caveat of being wary of the prosperity gospel, a temptation to converts from circumstances of poverty, we cannot underplay the growth of the church in the southern hemisphere at rapid rates, whilst the church in the West is declining in many cases. We also need to be aware of falling into negative paradigms, when we lose hope. The early church grew for a number of reasons, emanating from an experience of the Holy Spirit and repentance (turning to Jesus), building a strong community focus and above all keeping prayer at the heart of their life together. Prayers were answered miraculously, and signs and wonders were normative.

As the division between rich and poor increases in the modern world, David Bosch suggests that the church's mission could be countercultural and that through our radical discipleship, we could be agents of God's transformation, to create a just world based upon the principles of the kingdom of God:

> If rich Christians today would only practice solidarity with poor Christians – let alone the billions of poor people who are not Christians – this in itself would be a powerful missionary testimony and a modern day fulfilment of Jesus' sermon in Nazareth . . . As was the case in Jesus' own ministry, those in pain are to be liberated, the poor cared for, the outcasts and rejected brought home, and all sinners offered forgiveness and salvation.[17]

The early church did share everything but it did not become a club or an inward-looking sect. This is a great warning to the church today. There is a real danger of entrenching ourselves into ghettos, remaining inward-looking, maintaining what we have, rather than keeping our missionary zeal alive. The early church was outward-looking and missional from the beginning. It relied solely on the guidance and supernatural power of the Holy Spirit to enable the Christian community to grow significantly in numbers. About 3,000 are added to their number right from the outset. Growth came as a result of dependency on the Holy Spirit. A number of elements contributed to the church's remarkable growth: deep prayer and worship, sacrificial fellowship (putting the needs of others and of the community above their own needs), sharing food and Holy Communion. Most radically, 'All the believers were together and had everything in common. They sold property and possessions to give to anyone who had need' (2:44–45). The result was phenomenal growth, spiritual and numerical, and signs and wonders. 'And the Lord added to their number daily those who were being saved' (2:47). The Greek word for fellowship is *koinonia*. It is more holistic than just meeting together and encompasses sharing at two levels: in prayer and worship; sharing food and other possessions.[18]

They seemed to have little interest in material possessions or property, except to provide the necessities to live; it was as if they had been transported to a new non-material spiritual state. Again, in Acts 4:32–35 Luke writes about the communal life of the early church, which has grown yet again. The Holy Spirit had brought great unity: 'the believers were one in heart and mind' and their whole life was based upon their new, shared identity in Jesus. They pooled their possessions, as an expression of their love for each other – they were expressing that all things belonged to God, and therefore they should share them with their brothers and sisters. Of course, when personalities are involved, conflicts will always arise, but at this stage, the communal nature of the early church is something for us to reflect upon.

In socioeconomic terms, the way in which the early Christians lived out their lives was unheard of. Roman society was highly delineated: the rich, the property owners, were extremely wealthy, whilst the slaves quite literally had nothing. In Roman society, the concept of sharing outside your own family was unknown; the sharing of everything, even selling all one's possessions was radical and inconceivable. It is not entirely clear of what class of people the early church consisted, but given descriptions of the power of the Holy Spirit, it is more than likely that the whole spectrum of people were reached. That means that the church consisted of the wealthy, the property owning, widows, the artisans, even slaves.

Luke asks the question: how can we claim to be in Christ Jesus, united by the Spirit, if some of our members suffer because of poverty, lack of opportunity or don't have food on their plates? How can we see ourselves as brothers and sisters in Christ if some are homeless, whilst others have so much? The early church forfeited their own comfort and ownership of property for the common good. They lived out Jesus' teaching to 'Sell your possessions and give to the poor. Provide purses for yourselves that will not wear out, a treasure in heaven that will never fail, where no thief comes near and no moth destroys. For where your treasure is, there your heart will be also' (Luke 12:33–34). This remains a very radical message to Christians today, as the church consists of a whole spectrum of people, and considerable human need.

In our individual age, the church can offer real community

A friend of ours is a leader of a community group in a deprived multi-faith area in London. The way this group operates is to form communities of people, in this case living on an estate, sharing meals together, praying and worshipping, but above all getting involved in the local community, immersing themselves in it, living incarnationally.

This model of creating community originates in countries such as India and the Philippines, where members of the organisation live in the slums, building relationships with locals in their context. They set out to be deliberately different to the traditional mission paradigm, which tends to provide facilities for beneficiaries, top-down. Instead, involvement takes place through relationship and context.

In London, the community are involved with such activities as hosting a weekly evening for their friends and neighbours with a 'bring-and-share' meal and games, crafts, discussion, watching a film together; running a community garden in partnership with a Christian environmental charity; supporting friends and neighbours by helping with job applications, hospital appointments, legal issues etc.; volunteering at toddler groups, soup kitchens and shelters for homeless people run by local churches; leading a Bible study group for people on the edge of church.

The community leader told me, 'Our vision is to be an incarnational community in a deprived area. To be a community means relocating to an area, to be a light in that place, to reach out to our neighbours. The advantages of being a community are that we can support and encourage one another towards mission. I value the rhythm of worship, eating together, sharing support and fellowship. We encourage each other on our faith journeys. On the other hand, if you're a missional community, you can become inward-looking; not everyone comes to community "sorted", and this can distract from mission. By relocating, you can be a bit "top-down", as there is a gap between you and the local community. We relate to our community by "getting out there", chatting to people; we've networked with other organisations, e.g. Christians Against Poverty/children's centres/food banks. We get involved. For one year we were just "being" – not suggesting anything, just listening.'

This illustrates that community can be difficult too, but it provides a model of how we can rethink the church to be a community, rather than a number of disparate individuals accessing a service which is provided for them. This can be costly, but in the inner-city context people need to be there for some time, sacrificing what they find familiar to stand with the marginalised.

A suburban church in a city found itself linked with a church plant on a deprived estate, called The Centre. The seventies estate now includes a wide range of races, religions and nationalities – English, Somali Muslims, Eastern Europeans from orthodox and Muslim backgrounds, Arabs and Asian Muslims, Asian Hindus and Sikhs are all represented. The population density is very high. The statistics provide a picture of the estate and highlight the issues and challenges facing the residents: 21 per cent of the population are single parents, and only 29 per cent are in any form of employment. One third of the residents have no formal qualifications. The church leaders say, 'The Centre is a church for people who don't want to go to "church". We realised that people couldn't wait to get to see Jesus because he was dynamic, exciting and challenging. These are not words that most people would use to describe church today.'

They continue: 'Our desire is to get away from the formal, traditional style of church. That is not to say there is anything wrong with church like that – all we are saying is, there are plenty of churches like that and we don't want to be imitators, we would rather be innovators. If people prefer a more formal service, there are plenty of churches to choose from. However, we have discovered that there are not many alternatives. After asking the people on the estate what they would like for a service, we have decided that our services will be short, lively and relevant to everyday life. It is our prayer and hope that God will use us to bring back the sense of excitement for going to church and following Jesus that people had when Jesus walked this earth.'

Here is an example of a vision to create community in an area of diverse need. There is a sense of creating a radical, worshipping community that is relevant to the people it serves. This will provide a sense of community and a safe haven for those who attend. People living isolated lives, often far from home, will find a place to make friends, to deepen their faith or to find faith for the first time, to be listened to, to be cared for pastorally and be prayed for. The practical helps comes through the social projects, which also provide a sense of community, of linking people together and reducing the sense of being isolated.

Wesley Lane Chapel perceived that there were a number of isolated, elderly people, often living alone. A church member had a vision for a weekly event to create community for such people. Funding was sought to set up a lunch club, as there was a community hall attached to the church. Invitations were sent out, and gradually this became a popular event. As one user said, 'It's always lovely here. The helpers are so nice. We get a hot meal, and time to chat. Last week a lady came and showed us old photos of the town. We couldn't stop talking about the good old days.' The project was able to provide some simple activities, board games and excursions. A Holy Communion service was held before the lunch club, and some started to attend. An elderly man came to a living faith and said how much he loved the church. At the age of seventy-eight, he became a full member of the church and was very much loved by the congregation. This project provided a sense of community for the isolated and lonely. The church saw a need and responded, showing Christian love and reaching out with Jesus' love.

In the next chapter, we witness a further sign of the kingdom – a miraculous healing. The man healed is a disabled beggar – a person with no rights or dignity. We will reflect on the challenges facing the church in our contemporary much-divided society.

Action

- Consider the multicoloured, dramatic events of the first Pentecost. What were the fruits?
- Read through Acts 2, discerning signs of the Holy Spirit breaking down barriers of race and language.
- Reflect on Genesis 11 and Acts 2. How do you interpret the notion of Babel inverted? What does this mean for mission in today's society?
- Do you agree that churches attract similar people? What might be done to build more diverse communities of Christian faith? Who is left out at your church?
- Spend time pondering on Acts 2:42–47 and the priorities of the early church. What challenges you?

Endnotes

1. www.willy-brandt-biography.com/politics/german-unity.
2. I. Howard Marshall and D. Peterson (eds), *Witness to the Gospel: The Theology of Acts* (Grand Rapids, MI: William B. Eerdmans, 1998), p. 352.
3. R.C. Tannehill, *The Narrative Unity of Luke–Acts: A Literary Interpretation* (Minneapolis, MN: Fortress Press, 1990, p. 28.
4. Marshall and Peterson, *Witness to the Gospel*, p. 166.
5. Tannehill, *Narrative Unity*, p. 30.
6. Tannehill, *Narrative Unity*, p. 36.
7. Charles Parham, *The Latter Rain*, quoted in W.K. Kay and Ann Dyer (eds), *Pentecostal and Charismatic Studies* (London: SCM, 2004), p. 10.
8. Kay and Dyer, *Pentecostal and Charismatic*, p. 11.
9. Kay and Dyer, *Pentecostal and Charismatic*, p. 12.
10. Kay and Dyer, *Pentecostal and Charismatic*, p. 14.

11. Kay and Dyer, *Pentecostal and Charismatic*, p. 14.
12. Kay and Dyer, *Pentecostal and Charismatic*, p. 15.
13. Cecil Frances Alexander (1818–95), 'All Things Bright and Beautiful'.
14. Charles Wesley (1707–88), 'Love Divine, All Loves Excelling'.
15. Kay and Dyer, *Pentecostal and Charismatic*, p. 15.
16. Tannehill, *Narrative Unity*, p. 44.
17. David J. Bosch, *Transforming Mission* (New York: Orbis, 1991), p. 118.
18. Ben Witherington III, *The Acts of the Apostles, a Socio-Rhetorical Commentary* (Grand Rapids, MI: William B. Eerdmans, 1998), p. 160.

3
Inside Out – Radical Healing

The woman answered, 'I am surprised that you ask me for a drink! You are a Jew and I am a Samaritan woman!' (Jews have nothing to do with Samaritans.

(John 4:9, ERV)

The Samaritan woman in John 4 was not permitted to draw water from the same well as the Jews, as she was considered unclean. My mother, growing up in India in the 1930s, told me about the Dalits, who were not allowed to use the same wells as the higher caste Hindus, and sometimes had to sweep away their footprints so that Brahmins would not be contaminated through stepping into a Dalit's footprint. The Dalits, as they prefer to be known, are regarded as untouchable by much of Indian society, even though caste discrimination is outlawed. Dalit means 'crushed, broken and oppressed'. Tragically, the many Christians who converted from a Dalit background have found themselves discriminated against. The Dalit theologians look to Jesus as the liberator of an oppressed, poor and outcast people.

In Acts 3, Peter and John encountered someone who was very much an outcast, someone who was oppressed and having to beg for their very basic human needs. Peter and John saw he was in need of physical and emotional healing, and that his healing would lead to him being liberated from his condition. Let's take a closer look at Peter and John's powerful encounter with this disabled beggar, and see how Roman society was organised in terms of social class. We will then look at ways in which churches today are responding to the needs of class, powerlessness and poverty, particularly though the concept of 'regeneration' of communities, which has a spiritual concept at its heart.

A healing encounter

One day, Peter and John were on their way to the Temple at 3 p.m. to pray and praise God, and no doubt to share the love of Jesus with anyone who would listen. They were on that kind of high that church leaders encounter when they are full of the Spirit, and full of enthusiasm, spurred on by their witness and multitudes experiencing the love, power and transformation of Jesus.

I have experienced this on an inner-city Alpha course, where a group including Sri Lankan Buddhists, asylum seekers, Pentecostal Africans and middle-class whites met together. Suddenly, during a session about the Holy Spirit, the power of God was unleashed, and the group in its entirety experienced the power of the Holy Spirit in their lives, some falling prostrate on the floor. There was overwhelming joy – the joy of the Holy Spirit released. People were shedding tears of joy. This was a heaven-meets-earth moment, and it remains a great encouragement. At other times, I hold on to Jesus' parable of the lost sheep (Luke 15:1–7) and take joy in the one lost sheep that is found. Nothing much seems to be happening. But be encouraged by the small miracles. Charismatics in the inner city or on estates cannot really follow the models of 'mega churches'; everywhere is unique. We are called to seek God's vision and respond to the Holy Spirit's prompting.

This is exactly what Peter and John did. They were walking by, and a man lame from birth – we would call him 'physically disabled' today – was being carried to the Temple gate, with the explicit purpose of begging for alms. This was his only means of survival – there was no Disability Discrimination or Equality Act then. As in much of the world today, he was at the mercy of his family, or he had to beg in order to survive. People who loved him would carry him every day to the Beautiful Gate. As someone who was disabled, he would not have been able to enter the Temple.

When he got to his spot by the gate, he saw Peter and John on their way into the Temple, so he seized his opportunity and asked them for money. What happened next he could never have expected. Peter responded, 'I've got no money today,' as one would probably tell the tenth *Big Issue*-seller of the day. But Peter and John did not move away, for they saw this man, with all his frailty, all his pain, all his disability, created in the image of God and part of God's kingdom purposes. Full of the Holy Spirit, Peter took the man's hand, commanding him to get up and walk in the name of Jesus. Immediately, his feet and ankles were healed – made strong, and whole – and he jumped up and began to walk and jump, praising God. He recognised that it was the power of God that had healed him.

A miracle took place: the man experienced God's healing touch and was converted. John Wimber calls this 'power evangelism'. This had a knock-on effect, as others saw this miracle and were 'filled with wonder and amazement'. Wimber argues that in the West we have used reason alone to persuade people to come to Christ. Wimber contends that Acts tells another story: 'Rarely was church growth attributed to preaching alone [in the book of Acts].'[1] He lays great store in the power of healing and the miraculous to demonstrate that the kingdom of God is here. We are to go out into the world with the power of the Holy Spirit.

Healing linked to evangelism is an essential part of God's kingdom. Recently the church has grasped again the power of healing those outside the church – with such movements as Healing on the Streets, when Christians pitch up on market stalls, outside football grounds, or at car boot sales and offer prayer for healing. There have been numerous testimonies of people finding faith and healing as a result. The church is reminded that it needs to go out, to look outside of its own walls, and meet people where they are. This is the essence of the New Testament church and its phenomenal growth: ordinary people saw the signs and wonders; they witnessed the supernatural power of the Holy Spirit.

I wholeheartedly agree with this, but I am asserting that the kingdom of God is, at its heart, about the creation of justice, meeting the needs of the poor and excluded in every sense. I pose a different question: who was this man who was healed, and why did Luke choose to put this example of an outcast as the first healing in Acts? Philip Esler provides a detailed explanation of the way society was socially ordered by the Romans in its provinces in the first century after Christ.[2] There were three variables of economic class, and which class you belonged to determined not only your status in society, your access to wealth and means of production but also your social status within society and the power you held by virtue of your class.

The aristocrats and the dregs – Roman provincial society

The top echelons of Roman society in its provinces were the 'aristocracy', with the emperor at the pinnacle. These were landowners, although they normally resided in the cities; they owned vast country estates, worked by slaves. The slaves they owned were treated as their property; the aristocracy profited from others and enjoyed great status. Here was a sector of society, a social class who were extremely wealthy – their average salary was between 25,000 and 250,000 Denarii, whereas a worker would earn one Denarius pro rata. There was a massive difference in wealth. The aristocracy enjoyed great status and power. Amongst their rank were the senators and other leading civil figures. They enjoyed great luxury, and had distinctive, no doubt designer clothes and reserved seats, for example in the theatre or at the games. Economically, they made huge profits, as many of their workers were slaves and required no salaries. We are already seeing what a divided society this was.

The rest of Roman society were lumped together as the *humiliatives* (*humiliores*), which apparently translates as 'filth or dregs', which is how they were seen by the aristocracy. Among these were the more skilled workers: the artisans, the merchants (some of whom were better off), who were more socially organised, although still looked down on. Then there were the unskilled workers, who often relied upon day labour. But no work meant no food. Housing was often in piled-high tenement blocks, which were cramped and insanitary. This class included the blind, the physically disabled, as in Luke's healing story, and the mentally disturbed.[3] As we have seen, their only means of surviving was through begging or through the support of their families; technically they were free, i.e. not slaves, but they were at the mercy of others. Sometimes the rich would donate wheat to the poor, but they wanted prestige and honour in return. This is reminiscent of the Pharisees who paid to the Temple funds but wanted everyone to notice. Today, it is the equivalent of saying, 'I will donate to your church building fund but I want my name on a plaque.' Jesus was critical of the motivations of such giving, and Luke reports in his gospel that Jesus commended the widow who sacrificially gave everything she had as an example to follow (Luke 21:1–4).

Right at the bottom in Roman society were slaves, who apparently accepted their lot. They had no rights and were seen as property. They kept the whole infrastructure of the empire going at little cost, and therefore at maximum profit. They could be freed, and some freed slaves made a good living for themselves. There are numerous references to slaves in the New Testament, highlighting that they were a definitive section of the society at the time. In the most remarkable account, Onesimus the slave is converted to Christianity, in Paul's epistle to Philemon. Paul asked Philemon in a letter to forgive Onesimus, as he had run away, and to accept him as a fellow Christian and as a beloved brother. Slaves did convert, and through conversion may have secured release. Esler explains that all strata of society converted, but after AD 70 – after the Roman conquest of Palestine – thousands of slaves were scattered around the East.[4] Following conversion, the Christians of the Lucan community will have paid for the release of the debts of the slaves, in Luke's own words, 'to set the oppressed free' (Luke 4:18). The healed man came from this stratum of society – a man without rights and dignity, depending on scraps thrown to his feet.

In fact, people from every strata were converting, and in such a highly hierarchical and structured society, this was causing major issues in the Christian community. 'It is inevitable that God-fearers had been socialised to accept the stratification that affects society.'[5]

For Luke, this is an area where challenge was needed, for his vision of God's kingdom is one where all are accepted and there are no human-made barriers. As Esler elucidates:

> That the Lucan gospel imposes on the rich an indispensable requirement, quite at odds with the social values of their own society, to provide the destitute with food and other necessities of life in this world sounds like a death knell over all theology as affected by middle-class bias, to present salvation as a reality reserved for the individual in the afterlife.[6]

We are challenged, in our reading of Acts, that the socioeconomic issues are explicit and deserve close attention.

A divided society

The man healed by Peter and John became empowered, and his life changed from being at the mercy of others to being independent. Peter and John prayed for him for healing, but this healing was more than physical – it was spiritual, emotional and social. Suddenly he became empowered: empowered to work, empowered to make his own decisions, empowered to proclaim Christ.

We too live in a divided society. The poor remain overlooked and suffer through powerlessness, becoming pawns through successive changes in government policy. One of the most important results of the establishment of food banks is that it has put hidden poverty in plain sight and the need for action on the agenda. In this sense, the presence of food banks among us, even in the most affluent areas of the UK, opens the eyes of people to need and to the vulnerability and poverty of others in their midst. The fact that churches are responding to the challenge through opening and supporting food banks shows that holistic mission is being put into action, loving and serving people without judging them, and challenging unjust structures by being efficient at addressing social injustice. In this sense, food banks are subversive instruments which challenge everyone, including we who are comfortable Christians, to start to think about the possibility that our assumption that 'that could never happen to me' could move to 'that could be me next week'.

In 1985, the now much-quoted report *Faith in the City* was published. Although in many ways now dated, the pertinent issues raised remain the same. The report expressed serious concern about what was happening in British inner-city and outer council housing estate communities and highlighted the massive social divisions in society. The *Faith in the City* report urged the church to get involved in the concerns of 'Urban Priority Areas':

> What are now called urban priority areas are districts of specially disadvantaged character. They are places which suffer from economic decline, physical decay, and social disintegration. These factors interlock and together they describe multiple and relative deprivation . . . Such is the UPA, constituting a different Britain, whose people are prevented from entering fully into the mainstream of the normal life of the nation.[7]

Faith in the City positively recommended that the local church should get involved in shaping their community, and reflect the threefold approach of promoting flourishing, mediating tension and bringing hope.

The report actively encouraged the local church to be more committed to work in their area and with other local organisations such as the police, schools, councils and other voluntary groups. They recognised that 'definitions and methods may differ', but the idea of generating some 'sense of community' remains of value and is generally agreed to be desirable.[8] The report argued that the church must work with the disadvantaged, rather than for them. It mentions 'community work as a legitimate lay ministry . . . integrally linked to discipleship and worship'.[9] A change of culture had begun to regenerate, spiritually and physically, inner-city and estate churches. It actively promoted a local, outward-looking church that seeks to participate in the transforming of its neighbourhood. Paid community workers were commended to work with other community leaders to 'foster a sense of shared attitudes and strengthen the experience of human esteem and belonging'.[10]

Move on three decades. Nowadays, simply providing community workers is not enough – physical and spiritual transformation must be at the heart of any project. Recently *The Poverty and Social Exclusion Network* reported on the scandal of food banks. Reporting on the Trussell Trust, a Christian charity running food banks in the UK, they stated that 355,000 people received food parcels from its food banks between April and September 2017 – more than the number given out during the whole of the previous year. It says the increase was driven largely by hardship caused by benefit delays, welfare reform and low pay – and that the problem of hunger is getting worse. Chris Mould, executive chair of the Trust, said: 'The level of food poverty in the UK is not acceptable. It's scandalous and it is causing deep distress to thousands of people. The time has come for an official and in-depth inquiry into the causes of food poverty and the consequent rise in the usage of food banks.'[11]

In many council wards, churches work together to provide food banks, out of a biblical mandate to feed the hungry. The Westwood Food Bank in the Midlands was driven by local Christians who wanted to respond to hunger in their own area. It is ecumenical and relies on volunteers. Churches collect food, e.g. one church promoted BOGO – buy one and give one – rather than get something for free. These are then taken to a store, in one of the churches, and packages made up. Because of the huge need, sadly people cannot just turn up, but referrals are made from professionals, e.g. police and GPs, who can issue vouchers. Vouchers can be cashed in for food. At the Westwood Food Bank people are offered tea, a snack and time to chat if they so desire. Here is an example of Christians responding to poverty and inequality on their doorstep.

The recent report *Food Banks – A Theological Reflection*[12] researched the reason why people access food banks. The rising cost of living, changes to the benefit system and a delay in receiving benefits has resulted in the safety net of the welfare system, intended to assist the UK's poorest people, '[seemingly] to have developed more and more holes through which people now fall into extreme difficulty'. This includes many working people.

Linda ran a Christian food bank and shared this moving encounter:

In Acts 3:6, Peter gives us a paradigm for remembering that spiritual matters are more important than silver or gold. Those attending the food bank desperately needed physical sustenance. What was more difficult was training the volunteer workforce to move out of their comfort zone to talk, chat, and possibly to pray with those that came through our doors. My firm belief was that we had to be distinguishable from other food banks; no other voice was going to speak into their spiritual lives, and practical solutions without spiritual solutions seemed to deny the comprehensiveness of the gospel call.

The food bank operations were therefore re-modelled to ensure that collecting food was just one aspect of someone's visit to us. I saw Christ in each person arriving at the food bank, so our aim was to treat every person as if they were Christ himself. The process was designed to facilitate maximum care of each person.

Thinking back now, the remarkable thing was the answers to prayer. It was the answers to prayer that mostly led people into faith, and deeper into faith. People would share their stories, their difficulties; we would ask them what they would like us to pray for, and then we simply prayed for what they had asked – with them, there and then, over tea and biscuits.

One lady came in with her young children, and having collected her food shared with us how her husband had not been able to find work for over a year. He was now depressed as he felt he couldn't provide for his family. Her mental health was also affected, as she lived in fear of losing her home. She had delayed using the food bank as she knew he wouldn't like it, but the children were hungry and there was no food, so she had finally come to see us.

Having collected her food, we asked her if we could pray for anything, and she simply said, a job for her husband. She was back for more food the following week, her excitement obvious – her husband had unexpectedly got a job, and once he received his first pay packet she wouldn't need to return for more food. Her excitement and her new-found faith were contagious, and she was eager to share her experiences with everyone at the food bank that day, volunteers and visitors alike.

Poverty is a real issue, which is, if anything, getting worse. A recent report revealed that:

- 14 million people live in poverty in the UK – over 20 per cent of the population.
- One in eight working people, 3.7 million people, live in poverty, often on zero hours contracts.
- 40 per cent of working-age adults with no qualifications are living in poverty.
- Nearly half on the lowest incomes (3.2 million working-age people) spend more than one third of their income on housing.
- Food and energy bills take up a larger share of incomes. Over 4 million are not properly fed.
- 2.2 million of the poorest households have 'problem debt'.
- Around 2.3 million people cannot afford a pension.[13]

Regenerate
St Agnes' Church felt called to be involved in the regeneration of its community. Regeneration can be understood as God breathing new life into the community, empowering the community towards wholeness and fulfilment. Of course, just improving material condition is not

an end in itself spiritually, but a church involved in its community is wrestling with fundamental questions of how to be salt and light (Matthew 5:13–16) amidst the suffering and darkness of all that is going on around them.

St Agnes' is a church on a large estate in an area of severe multiple deprivation. The minister and members of the church community (most of whom lacked confidence) prayed and sought God's guidance about how they could serve their community. To begin, they conducted a community audit. Out of this they found the most pressing need was for youth work. Council-run services came and went; there was no consistency. Antisocial behaviour was on the up, and there was strong feeling that positive activities for young people on the estate were needed. The church then responded that they would like to raise funds to employ a youth worker, who would work with the community to set up a youth project. The church leaders, with a little assistance, began the process of fundraising. Remarkably, after two years, exactly the right amount had come in, and a worker was employed.

The worker ran a church-based youth group, as well as a youth drop-in at the community centre. A number of volunteers were recruited, and the project had a strong Christian ethos, although it did not seek to proselytise. The youth worker also ran mentoring sessions in a local high school, through which one person started coming to church, and then to faith. Gradually his mother and sister also came to faith, his mother through an Alpha course. The community were positive about the youth work, and gradually the position of the church in the community changed – the church became increasingly the central axis for any initiative on the estate.

The minister and youth/community worker were invited to be key players in the estate regeneration initiative. One successful regeneration initiative was the 'Link-Up' project, which aimed to build social capital on the estate. This brought together key partners: the church, a youth project, a play centre, a 'better health' representative, a Muslim after-school club and an estate community group. This group intentionally broke down barriers with the aim of providing events that would improve peoples' lives on the estate. It was very much community-led, and received funding for projects through an innovative council fund aimed at empowering residents. Events included a fun day, which was extremely popular. There was food from around the globe, children's entertainers, five-a-side football and the obligatory bouncy castle. Community education, e.g. on fire safety and on diet was provided, all done in a fun way. There was also a trip to the seaside, with full coaches. One of the organisers reported how moving this was, as many of the children had never seen the sea. For the church at the hub of this initiative, it was a strong way to build links into the local community. Through the process of the church becoming better known on its estate, two families came for baptism of their children, and one ended up staying in the church, coming to a living faith.

This involvement of serving the community through joining up groups for the common good is an example of building social capital:

> Social capital can be defined quite simply as a set of informal values or norms shared among members of a group that permits co-operation among them. If members of the group come to expect that others will come to behave reliably and honestly, then they will come to trust one another. Trust is like the lubricant that makes the running of any group or organisation more efficient.[14]

Reciprocity and trust are the keys to social capital. Social capital operates on different levels – the example I have given is of 'bridging social capital'. As Ann Morisy explains: 'Bridging social capital extends trust to beyond one's network, and encourages smooth relations with strangers . . . bridging social capital leads to broadening of people's identities because it requires journeying out to engage with the stranger'.[15]

In theological terms, it is the journey of a church out of its comfort zone into its wider environment: creating understanding, building bridges, sharing resources. In Acts, the apostles and the followers of Jesus were constantly on a journey: a literal journey to spread Jesus and a spiritual journey, as they found themselves in new situations, asking the Holy Spirit how they should respond. Ann Morisy goes on to explain how a lack of social capital in poor communities leads to the very real demographic of a 'geographically based underclass' characterised by a negative subculture. A cycle takes place: gangs form, they are involved in antisocial behaviour, established residents feel insecure and move out. New residents move in, but do not have the same level of commitment to the area, so the area is perceived as 'going downhill'.[16]

The whole regeneration process in the 2000s sought to address these issues. Much good work has been done, helped considerably by positive government financing. This era has now ended, and it has become much more difficult to fund the many excellent projects churches run for and in partnership with their communities. As services and funding are cut, it will become much more difficult to create positive, transforming communities; the social capital that had been built up is again being diminished and the gap left will be enormous. This is an acute challenge for the church.

The regeneration process, which I was very closely involved in, empowered local residents to prioritise and manage the improvement of their community. As Ann Morisy notes, the church has a major role to play in transforming their communities:

The fact that churches have been present in communities for decades, if not centuries, counts for something. No other agency will have the voice and depth of history that the Church represents, and the local churches must harness, and be allowed to harness, this asset wisely and generously, because it cannot easily be replicated.[17]

In the next chapter, we will see how this act of healing resulted in huge spiritual opposition for Peter and John, when they found themselves on trial for following the Holy Spirit. We will then consider how spiritual opposition has led to a lack of engagement with Christianity in many urban settings and outer estates. We need to be proactive in seeking God's growth.

Action

- Think about the healing of someone socially excluded in Acts 3 – why is this important to Jesus and his followers? Look for examples of healings of the socially excluded in Luke's gospel – what does this tell us about Jesus?
- Who are the socially excluded today?
- In your area, can you think about specific social needs and how you may be able to build bridges into your community?
- Are there community events or community forums you can be part of, to work together for the common good or regeneration of the community?

Endnotes

1. John Wimber, *Power Evangelism* (New York: Harper & Row, 1986), p. 118.
2. P.F. Esler, *Community and Gospel in Luke–Acts: The Social and Political Motivations of Lucan Theology* (Cambridge: Cambridge University Press, 1987), p. 172.
3. Esler, *Community and Gospel*, p. 172.
4. Esler, *Community and Gospel*, p. 183.
5. Esler, Community and Gospel p. 199.
6. Esler, *Community and Gospel*, p. 199.
7. The Archbishop of Canterbury's Commission on Urban Priority Areas, *Faith in the City: A Call for Action by Church and Nation* (London: Church House, 1985), p. 9.
8. *Faith in the City*, p. 57.
9. *Faith in the City*, p. 288.
10. *Faith in the City*, p. 288.
11. www.benefitsandwork.co.uk/news/2404-charity-calls-for-official-inquiry-as-food-bank-use-triples-in-a-year#comment-1212 (accessed 16.1.18).
12. *Food Banks – A Theological Reflection*, https://www.churchofengland.org/sites/default/files/2017-11/MTAG%20Mission%20and%20Food%20Banks.pdf (accessed 16.1.18).
13. See https://www.jrf.org.uk/report/uk-poverty-2017 (accessed 10.10.17).
14. Francis Fukuyama, *The Great Disruption* (London: Profile, 1999), p. 16.
15. Ann Morisy, *Journeying Out* (London: Continuum, 2004), p. 50.
16. Morisy, *Journeying*, p. 51.
17. Morisy, *Journeying*, p. 51.

4
The Church Grows, Despite Opposition

Accustom yourself to look first to the dreadful consequences of failure; then fix your eye on the glorious prize which is before you; and when your strength begins to fail, and your spirits are well-nigh exhausted, let the animating view rekindle your resolution, and call forth in renewed vigour the fainting energies of your soul.

William Wilberforce[1]

Seeking God's guidance, discerning his will and then stepping out in faith can lead Christians to pain, demoralisation and opposition. William Wilberforce underwent thirty years of persistent opposition to his anti-slavery bill before it was finally passed in 1807. In Acts 4, we have the first major account of how the apostles suffered opposition and persecution for obeying God. This is a theme that will recur throughout the book of Acts and the epistles. The apostles persevered despite opposition to spread the message of Jesus through acts of love and through preaching Christ crucified.

In this chapter, we will look at the trial of Peter and John, and at how opposition led not to decline but to growth in the early church. In today's climate, there is much talk about church decline, especially in the 'tough places' of outer estates and inner cities. Recently I drove through an outer estate of 30,000 people, built about fifty years ago. I saw the derelict shell of a once nonconformist church, and a 'for sale' sign on another Anglican church. The church can struggle in the face of widespread opposition for a vast array of reasons: apathy, individualism, a lack of perceived relevance and being judged to be out of touch. Decline is common but, if we take note of the early church, it should not be normative. We will look at the whole question of church growth in tough places. It can be achieved, in the Spirit's power.

Mission is holistic – it includes spiritual and numerical growth as well as the transformation of unjust structures through Christian love in action. Secondly, if mission does not take place, the church will cease to be a credible and prophetic presence in many deprived communities. Real transformation takes place when individuals and communities encounter the living Christ.

On trial

Acts 4: following the healing, Peter and John found themselves in big trouble with the Sanhedrin – this was a body which had not only the power of arrest but also the power to determine what type of public activity was permissible within Jerusalem. The Sanhedrin certainly did not permit public discourse about Jesus. Peter and John, of course, could not obey. They ended up being arrested and put in prison for the night. The next day, the rulers, the elders and teachers of the law – the Sanhedrin – met in Jerusalem and summoned Peter and John to be brought before them (Acts 4:5–7). They questioned the power of the Sanhedrin, who they saw as some kind of religious and political elite. Peter and John replied, 'Which is right in God's eyes: to listen to you, or to him? You be the judges! As for us, we cannot help speaking about what we have seen and heard' (Acts 4:19–20). Following God's will was paramount, so they found themselves in conflict with the Sanhedrin who they believed had exceeded their power.

The Sanhedrin was the Jewish supreme council, comprising seventy men, plus the high priest who served as its chair. Luke's list of those present includes the high priest and others of the high priest's family, suggesting that this body was close-knit and tightly controlled. The members came from the chief priests, scribes and elders. During the trial, Peter reminded the Sanhedrin that they were responsible for the crucifixion of Jesus and that salvation only comes through Jesus. Peter made clear that human beings cannot be saved through keeping the law and by closely following all its statutes. Peter proclaimed a message of grace, which Paul later summed up as: 'We . . . know that a person is not justified by the works of the law, but by faith in Jesus Christ. So we, too, have put our faith in Christ Jesus that we may be justified by faith in Christ and not by the works of the law, because by the works of the law no one will be justified' (Galatians 2:15–16). This was the new age: Peter's defence clarified that Jesus had risen, this could not be disputed; even though the Sanhedrin sanctioned his crucifixion, Jesus had defeated death and was now alive. He had sent his Spirit, with great power, to enable his work on earth to be done, and the lame man being healed was testimony to this.

Peter and John did not actually question the authority of the Sanhedrin. In his address, Peter addressed them respectfully, acknowledging their revered position in society: 'Rulers and elders of the people!' Peter and John were direct in their announcement that they were obeying God, not humans. They used extremely direct language in response to the charges against them; the Holy Spirit is given to those who are faithful in their obedience and witness. The Sanhedrin clearly had not received the Holy Spirit and it was to God's authority alone that the apostles would bow. The council were startled by their courage, particularly as they were 'unschooled ordinary men' (v. 13). For Luke, it was clearly the Holy Spirit who had empowered them with such boldness. Luke placed little value on the training in oratory and in the law that the leaders and teachers of the law had undergone. The gospel could be proclaimed by anyone, it was not merely for an educated elite.

Seeing this lack of subservience to their authority, the Sanhedrin desired their death – they were enraged at this seemingly anarchic conduct.[2] Furthermore, King Agrippa was set on killing Peter and so gained popularity through siding with the Sanhedrin. However, the healed man stood as an 'exhibit' in court, as a testimony of healing. Consequently, they could find no charge against Peter and John. When commanded 'not to speak or teach at all in the name of Jesus' they replied that they must obey God, not humans, and they must do what the Spirit led them to do, which was to testify to Jesus (vv. 19–20).

The church grows

Following opposition and persecution, Peter and John returned to the Christian community and reported back all that happened. No doubt the gathered Christians would have been fearful that their leaders could have been imprisoned or even sentenced to death. Their release greatly encouraged the early church, as once again it testified to the power of the resurrected Jesus over evil. At once, they responded in prayer. Firstly, they praised God the creator, as everything that happens on earth is due to his sovereignty. Next, they praised God's power as seen throughout history and acknowledged the death of Jesus at the hands of Herod, Pilate and the Jews. Then they prayed for even greater boldness and more miracles, to usher in God's reign. Finally, they called out to God, 'Stretch out your hand to heal and perform signs and wonders through the name of your holy servant Jesus' (v. 30). At this point, their prayer was answered and the earth shook: 'they were all filled with the Holy Spirit and spoke to word of God boldly.' The word 'boldly' is a recurring one, emphasising that the apostles and their converts had a specific mission to bring people to see their need for Jesus.

Growing churches in tough places

For some time now, with many years' experience of estate and inner-city ministry under my belt, I have been asking the question, 'Why do some churches in these contexts grow, whilst many do not?' In fact, this very question allowed me to undertake some research. In their book *Angels on the Walls*, an inspiring account of how one small church on a deprived outer estate of Birmingham grew, Wallace and Mary Brown emphasise the importance of every member ministry:

> The biblical model, however, is 'every member ministry'; a situation where all people who claim to be Christians are called to be the church. Therefore 'being church' is a corporate exercise. Of course, all churches need leadership, but so-called omnicompetent vicars . . . It was obvious our 'control' was limiting growth, yet how could

we develop every member ministry, especially when so many of our folk were from a disempowered background?[3]

The solution involves a level of risk-taking, so mission can happen, 'otherwise just hold on to what exists because it is safe.'[4]

The book ends with a plea for change. The authors write about a context of outer estates, where small churches are the norm. Social, spiritual and sociological change has led to a position where: 'The traditional Christian moral background has been plundered by post-modernism; one-parent families abound; on many estates gangs loiter on street corners, domestic violence escalates, drink dominates, children swear at passers-by and drugs are readily available.'[5]

In this situation the church, too, has lost its way, being seen as irrelevant to the vast majority of the local community:

A sort of stuffy club that 'tut tuts' at the modern lifestyle. As people use the church for occasional offices less, contact with the church is reduced to the extent that the church fades more and more into the background.[6]

The Browns' hilarious account of St Anybody's Church is very telling. It is cliquey, old-fashioned and irrelevant, holding on to the norms of the past rather than looking to the postmodern culture of today. Visitors feel they are intruding. There are powerful groups resisting change. Churches, the authors argue, need to engage with postmodern culture, which means they need to analyse, adapt and change. The alternative is a slow, unremitting death:

Yet that is not the way of the Spirit of God: he continually raises up prophetic signposts to each generation. The Father guides his people to speak meaningfully to every culture. Of course the message of the gospel does not change but it must be expressed to give understanding within cultural 'receiving zones.'[7]

The challenge is to bring about change creatively, not being afraid of adapting, being willing to take risks and move forward in the Holy Spirit's power. Change is not easy to manage, and congregations often do not like change. It takes time to transform the culture of a church; patience will be needed. Having a clear vision, a mission statement and knowing which direction we are going sets us well on the road to recovery.

The diagnosis

We do have a clear mandate from Jesus to 'go and make disciples of all nations' (Matthew 28:19), and small churches, as well as large ones, are challenged to show a willingness to be missionary. Assessing the health of a congregation provides a good way in. Churches are best seen as living organisms; like us, as human beings, they need to be healthy and striving towards wholeness in order to flourish. But, to continue this parallel, disease cannot be avoided; the challenge is *how* we respond to disease. As a starting point, congregations that are healthy are those which are willing to diagnose any disease, and seek to learn from the experience. In small churches, this is both pertinent and pivotal to growth: small churches that are unwilling to address disease, and accordingly are not in a healthy state, are unlikely to grow, and thereby will be unable to serve their community.

Perhaps the most significant research on understanding how different-sized churches operate in relation to church size is by Arlin Rothauge.[8] Rothauge has found the small church is best categorised as a family. This has both positive and negative connotations: the idea of family is good and wholesome, where people belong, but families can also be dysfunctional and closed systems, where outsiders can never fit in. Rothauge finds there are four key figures involved in the dynamic of small churches. Firstly, as the metaphor of family is used, there are strong parental figures, 'in control of the norms and changes in the family life', usually matriarch and patriarch figures. They are usually long-term members who have become established, quite literally, as the parental figures within this family dynamic. Like the parent, they will exercise much power, and ultimately any decision depends upon their approval.

As for the pastor in this situation, they 'will function as chaplain but not as the primal father [or mother]'.[9] They are seen as people to provide pastoral care, to be chaplain to the congregation. What may ensue is that much of the pastor's time is spent in frustration and in conflict with the patriarchs and matriarchs. As pastors tend to come and go, often staying no more than five to six years, small churches become tremendously resilient. This is positive in some ways, as it models very successfully lay involvement and lay leadership, but equally it is disadvantageous to growth, as there are definite stakeholders, people who hold power.

The final player in this dynamic is the 'gatekeeper' or 'welcome person'. The 'gatekeepers' serve the role of a warm, cheerful, welcoming person, who has a heart to reach out. The welcome person is the initial contact, but he or she is not sufficient to enable the new person to feel part of the church. Rothauge points out that

> the gatekeeper opens the door, but it is the patriarch and matriarch who sanction a place in the family for the newcomer. The method of assimilation is more like adoption than simple social acceptance. The adoption will take longer than social acceptance, but the eventual bond with the new church family will be very strong.[10]

This makes it very difficult for anyone to fit in; some may be adopted, others may be rejected.

In the following situation, a new minister, Sue (relatively young and in her first post), has arrived, full of new ideas and enthusiasm, to an outer estate church and community. In the interregnum (the time between ministers), the identified matriarch, the lay preacher, has been, whether consciously or not, taking on the role of the church leader, and has become seen as such by the congregation. She also commands high status within the community. She has decided which services to use and what music may be sung. Her husband, the organist, is very content with this situation, as he did not like the last minister's penchant for modern choruses.

The patriarch is the churchwarden (key elder), of many years, and is on the same wavelength as the matriarch, theologically and personally. The patriarch and his wife take charge of the order in the church, manage the community hall and the cleaning (which they do themselves as no one else can seem to do it right). Order is their domain, and no one dares move or spill anything. They have given years to this church and they treat it as their own home – in fact, it is effectively an extension of it. The welcome person is a similar age, a former elder, and the main Sunday school teacher. She is close to, and accepted by, the matriarch and patriarch but has a different personality, and a passion for church growth.

Early on, Sue reaches serious conflict with the patriarch. She spent time getting to know community leaders, and has introduced a toy library into the church building. Although this has been agreed, the patriarch and his wife attend every session and make the beneficiaries feel uncomfortable. They give out the aura of being in control, and undermine Sue, who is eager to build good relations with all who come in, as part of her witness.

Feeling undermined, Sue has a meeting with the patriarch. This does not go well and he refuses to back down from being present. The matriarch backs the patriarch; soon there are definite factions in the church. It is worth noting that in small churches, any difficulties show up publicly and quickly! The patriarch has some enemies, but they are afraid of upsetting him. These people side with Sue secretly but are not willing to be public about this. They fear being ostracised from the church family. Sue tries to reason with the patriarch that he is inhibiting her ministry and the mission of the church, and that she, as the leader, needs to be free to lead and seek God's fresh vision. After several no-win situations, eventually the patriarch agrees to step down as churchwarden, but not until Sue has had to enlist support from her more senior points of reference, and then he makes himself into a martyr. Sue and the matriarch find they can work together creatively, although tensions arise from time to time. It is the welcome person who helps bring healing into the church community; gradually healing takes place in the life of the church and Sue is able to minister in a more proactive, mission-focused way.

Moving on: a prognosis

If mission, in its widest sense, is not happening in a positive way and the minister is not functioning freely, then there are almost certainly interpersonal issues which need to be dealt with. This willingness to engage creatively is a sign of health – to seriously attempt to examine the disease and seek healing. Pastoral sensitivity is needed as, often, ministers become victims of those who are themselves chronically anxious; church leaders need to establish in themselves boundaries of what they consider unacceptable. Conflict is unpleasant, and something church leaders are generally unprepared for. However, if tackled positively, it can be liberating to the whole church and to God's mission as a whole. 'Responsible church leaders serve as models of a firm and assertive approach to conflict that is flexible but not floppy, compassionate but not sloppy *agape*, steady but not immovable.'[11]

Never underestimate the power of prayer! In countless situations, God has been able to bring change, so that key people step down, or people 'see the light' and are changed. A high level of patience is of course needed, and a desire to be tuned into God's voice and vision for the future of that church.

Assessing health: moving towards growth

After almost two decades of church growth theory, often imported from America, there has been a radical turnaround in thinking. Most influential in this process has been Christian Schwarz and his writing on *Natural Church Development* (NCD).[12] Schwarz maintains that just as there are principles of growth within nature, God has established principles by which churches grow. Our challenge is to discover and implement these principles; as we do, growth becomes natural, blessed by God. What is significant for small churches is Schwarz's finding that the largest churches are not necessarily the healthiest. And it is not necessarily right to emulate their patterns and programmes of doing things – this is not always appropriate for smaller churches, and can be demoralising. Those in smaller churches should know that they can be involved in quality ministry and community engagement without being beleaguered by size.

In the UK, Robert Warren's *The Healthy Churches' Handbook* is very helpful in enabling churches to engage with this vital process of identifying and addressing obstacles and impediments to growth.[13] Warren has established the following measures of a healthy church:

Energised by faith
Outward-looking focus
Seeks to find out what God wants
Faces the cost of change and growth
Operates as a community
Makes room for all
Does a few things and does them well

With the handbook, there is a questionnaire that can be utilised, that the whole congregation can fill in. The next stage is to collate the results; a simple visual presentation/bar graphs may be helpful. Following this, you can meet together, perhaps with a smaller group, for an afternoon away.[14] The purpose of this day is to get some feedback on the results of the survey, to celebrate strengths, and to begin to look in detail at ways in which the weaknesses can be overcome, as it shows which areas need to improve so that more growth can take place. Specific work in small groups on the obstacles to growth can lead to a positive way forward. It is possible to break down problematic areas within the life of the church into manageable steps towards creative solutions. There are, of course, no quick or easy answers, and change does take considerable time.

Looking outwards

At the Community Church, in a multicultural estate setting, the congregation completed a simplified version of the 'healthy churches' questionnaire – initially the year a new pastor arrived and again twelve months later. One area of weakness found was the fact that many people did not feel an active 'part' of the church. A solution the leadership group came up with was to move towards more participation – every-member ministry. They suggested a simple 'gifts questionnaire' could be drawn up for people to fill in, then the results could be collated and teams drawn up. The result was an almost complete culture shift. From there only being a few people involved in the life of the church, virtually everyone, including children, found they had a role to play. Spiritually, as a charismatic church, the whole body of Christ were invited to discover and use their spiritual gifts to build the kingdom of God.

The *Faith in the City* report urged an outward-looking focus to urban churches, which is even more timely today:

An effective UPA [Urban Priority Area] Church will not just be a local Church in the sense of reflecting local cultures and people in its membership, leadership, and styles of working. It will also be a Church which takes seriously the local realities of life as an integral part of its mission to UPAs and the whole of society. It will look outwards because God sends us out into the world. The alienation between Church of England and the majority of working-class people must cause us all to be greatly disturbed. Faced with such a situation the Church cannot persist in the way of self-preservation and that 'institutional self-interest' which so often preoccupies it. It has to move from the policies of maintenance to the outward-looking policies of mission.[15]

The community of the church also needs to hold a balance between a sense of belonging, whilst at the same time being 'transparent' and allowing people to see into the life of the church, the people and the community of faith. The mission of the church is its ability to reach out and interact with the community it finds itself in, whilst not losing its spiritual edge. I suggest it is not enough to run a mother and toddler group without immersing it in prayer, and discerning how the project will lead to people engaging with faith issues. Mission has to be the central motivation of the church, and churches that grow clearly have an outward-looking focus, as Warren has found. At the community church, they felt that they need to create a balance between spiritual growth, outward-looking focus and quality of relationships. The result has been significant numerical and spiritual growth.

At Trinity, another growing church in a very multi-faith area, encompassing Sikhs, Muslims, Hindus and Christians living in close proximity, a number of the congregation had a vision to engage with the local community and open wide their doors, so they prayed, researched and then started a playgroup. Within a relatively short time, it reached a large number of families outside the church – a whole cross-section of the community, including Hindus, Sikhs and a handful of Muslims. This playgroup had a significant impact on the community: it built bridges so that people came into the church building who otherwise would not have entered. The church also attempted to go out of its doors and into the neighbourhood, through holding a community fun day, with the result that many children and families now know the church and its members. Playgroup users are invited to special services such as the Harvest Festival. The project is prayed for by the church, and in the minister's words, 'Playgroup has a high profile on Sundays.' The key leaders of the playgroup are all church members – for ten years, a team of four people have seen this as their main ministry. They have been liberated by the Holy Spirit to serve, using their gifts.

As the early church grows, more and more ethical complexities come into play. In the next chapter we move on to scrutinise the corrupting hold of money: ways in which our society has become excessively materialistic, and how this impacts the materially poorest, in terms of debt and self-esteem.

Action

- Assess how healthy you think your church is, using the factors in this chapter. In *The Healthy Churches' Handbook* there are more detailed questionnaires.
- How do we deal maturely with conflict as Christians? Have a look at Matthew 18:15–17.
- Are there ways of supporting a church in a tough area (outer estate, inner city), ready to grow, but needing resources (people, support, prayer, not just finance)?
- Do you agree that running projects in the church building can lead to church growth? Maybe you could do some research locally to find out.
- Maybe spend some time finding out about the joys and struggles of ministry in tougher places.

Endnotes

1. https://www.goodreads.com/quotes/385815 (accessed 22.1.18).
2. R.J. Cassidy, *Society and Politics in the Acts of the Apostles* (Maryknoll, NY: Orbis, 1987), p. 40.
3. Wallace and Mary Brown, *Angels on the Walls* (Eastbourne: Kingsway, 2000), p. 191.
4. Brown and Brown, *Angels*, p. 191.
5. Brown and Brown, *Angels*, p. 239.
6. Brown and Brown, *Angels*, p. 241. 'Occasional offices' refers to funerals, weddings and baptisms.
7. Brown and Brown, *Angels*, p. 244.
8. Arlin J. Rothauge, *Sizing Up a Congregation for New Member Ministry* produced by the Education for Mission and Ministry Office by Seabury Professional Services, www.eastmich.org (accessed 27.7.15).
9. Rothauge, *Sizing Up*, p. 3.
10. Rothauge, *Sizing Up*, p. 5.
11. Arthur Paul Boers, *Never Call them Jerks* (Boulder Creek, CA: The Alban Institute, 1999), p. 5.
12. Christian A. Schwarz, *Natural Church Development: A Guide to Eight Essential Qualities of Healthy Churches* (St Charles, IL: ChurchSmart Resources, 1996).
13. Robert Warren, *The Healthy Churches' Handbook* (London: Church House Publishing, 2004).
14. For example, leadership team/PCC/church elders/a specially selected working group.
15. The Archbishop of Canterbury's Commission on Urban Priority Areas, *Faith in the City: A Call for Action by Church and Nation* (London: Church House, 1985), p. 75.

5
The Love of Money is . . .

To the eyes of a miser a guinea is more beautiful than the sun . . .
William Blake[1]

The hold of money can have a corrupting influence on all aspects of life
– the personal, the spiritual, the emotional and the social. In the New
Testament, Paul warns that 'the love of money is a root of all kinds of
evil. Some people, eager for money, have wandered from the faith and
pierced themselves with many griefs' (1 Timothy 6:10). In the parable
of the rich young ruler, the tragedy of the message lies in the rich young
man's inability to let go of his riches, which he worshipped above God:
'"If you want to be perfect, go, sell your possessions and give to the
poor, and you will have treasure in heaven. Then come, follow me."
When the young man heard this, he went away sad, because he had
great wealth' (Matthew 19:21–22).

Acts 5 begins with the rather brutal and alarming 'real-life parable'
of attempting to deceive God by holding back riches. The premise of
this short but startling narrative is that material possession can corrupt
both the mind and our human capacity to make moral judgements.
In this chapter we will look at the account of Ananias and Sapphira,
and explore how in our contemporary postmodern society, the gods
of mammon have led to a materialistic, highly divided society. Lack of
wealth has led to social problems, particularly debt and low self-image.
We will then look at some examples of how churches and projects are
dealing with these issues creatively.

Ananias and Sapphira
To put this account (Acts 5:1–11) into context, we begin with the
apostles' foundational theological understanding that all material

possessions of the Christian community are to be shared. The subtext is that everything we possess belongs to God, as elucidated in 1 Chronicles 29:11: 'Yours, LORD, is the greatness and the power and the glory and the majesty and the splendour, for everything in heaven and earth is yours. Yours, LORD, is the kingdom; you are exalted as head over all.' This is articulated in church services when the collection is brought forward. I do not believe that today, as we give our small offerings back to God, we fully grasp the meaning of this verse. But the early church did. They took it very literally, and at the heart of their community was the idea that everything they possessed should be given to the common pot, so that no one would be in need:

> All the believers were one in heart and mind. No one claimed that any of their possessions was their own, but they shared everything they had. With great power the apostles continued to testify to the resurrection of the Lord Jesus. And God's grace was so powerfully at work in them all that there was no needy person among them. For from time to time those who owned land or houses sold them, brought the money from the sales and put it at the apostles' feet, and it was distributed to anyone who had need.
>
> Acts 4:32–35

This is a very radical concept. In Greek society, the idea of reciprocity was at the heart of friendship: you gave gifts to someone you valued, but you would expect something back in return. Here, Luke's picture is one of generous love: because you love God, God is at work in your life, so you give your material possessions to alleviate the suffering of those who cannot otherwise survive. It was the apostles themselves who were charged with the distribution of goods, to ensure that no one was lacking human basics – food, accommodation, spiritual support. This continued until the task became too onerous, as the church had grown so large (Acts 6). We will look at this in the next chapter.

In Acts 4:36–37, Luke gives an example of 'Joseph, a Levite from Cyprus', known as Barnabas (son of encouragement), who sold a field and gave the proceeds to the apostles. Barnabas played a key role in spreading the gospel later, and in providing encouragement to the church to remain 'true to Christ', as they underwent persecution and difficulty. Barnabas' life had been transformed by his encounter with Jesus; he is described as 'a good man, full of the Holy Spirit and faith' (Acts 11:24), who brings many people to the Lord. He did not become caught up in the worship of material things and, in this instance, willingly gave up his land for the common good.

In contrast, Ananias and Sapphira are depicted as not being able to loosen the idolatrous hold money had upon them. They had clearly come to faith in Jesus, but when it came to their material possessions and wealth, they could not give it all up. What Luke highlights as their greatest sin was their lack of honesty and their selfishness. Their lack of faith prevented them from surrendering to the common good, and they overtly lied to the apostles and to God. Peter, prompted by the Holy Spirit, asked Ananias, 'How is it that Satan has so filled your heart that you have lied to the Holy Spirit and have kept for yourself some of the money you received from the land?' (Acts 5:3). The moral of this tale is a harsh one. Lying to the Holy Spirit resulted in instant death for both Ananias and his wife.

This raises an important issue: the pattern seems to have been to share everything in common, and certainly have a deep concern that the poor and outcasts were cared for. Ananias and Sapphira weakened their discipleship by lying to both God and people, and holding on to their wealth selfishly. Yet, the early church was a vibrant microcosm of society, reaching all sectors. There were rich, poor, wealthy landowners and dispossessed slaves. But all had a sense of community, of belonging together. Some wealthy people had large houses which they shared with the Christian community, so that they could worship together; this was a house church movement.

This is a difficult paradox for us today, and indeed for the church through its history. In our society, there is great discrepancy between churches in wealthy suburbs and those serving in areas of marked poverty. In the Church of England, there is system of 'share' – of sharing finance, whereby wealthier parishes may give more than is needed to their costs for ministry, so that parishes in poorer areas may be able to continue in mission and ministry by employing a minster (who, increasingly, is shared by two to three churches). Nevertheless, I am convinced that the majority of churchgoers do not understand how challenging yet fulfilling ministry can be in the inner city. There is still a tendency to want to keep the money to build up their own church – to employ more staff, have more youth workers and children's workers. Such opportunities would be so revitalising for churches in the inner-city and estate areas, but for most this is not a possibility – not a luxury they can afford. I hope that the wider church may begin to grasp that God's church is for all sectors of society and to see how we can share God's love with all.

Materialism today

Our postmodern culture today, with its strong emphasis on material possessions, appearance and fashion, has massive implications for those living in poverty. We will explore the implications of culture shifts for those who live in poverty, through the themes of debt and self-image, with examples of how Christians have begun to address these.

It is to the 1950s that the beginning of the consumer revolution may be traced back. The role of consumerism in current Western society is a central tenet in our postmodern society. Sociologist Zygmunt Bauman argues that we have become consumers rather than producers; so great is this shift that 'consumer conduct (consumer freedom geared to the consumer market) moves steadily into the position of, simultaneously, the cognitive and moral focus of life, the integrative bond of society, and the focus of systematic management'.[2] Furthermore, since the 1980s, the demise of traditional working-class industries and production, e.g. coal mines, cotton mills, the steel and shipbuilding industries, have led to an identity crisis in the traditional working class. Whole communities had been left without hope and purpose. Where I grew up, generation after generation had gone down t' pit, i.e. coal mining. Suddenly, whole swathes of the population found themselves without work, already suffering huge emotional trauma from the miners' strike of 1984. Drug use became prevalent, and crime increased. Many people became dependent on benefits, and lost hope and purpose. Marriages broke down.

Nowadays, consumerism defines identity; it defines who we are. Consumerism marks the search for social approval through lifestyle: the need to define ourselves and be accepted by our peers through the labels we wear, what we drink, eat, furnish our homes with, etc. Shopping becomes the 'membership requirement' of our social grouping and therefore says 'we belong', along with a keeping-up-with-the-Patels-type rivalry to mark out our position in society. 'There is pressure to spend: on the *social level*, the pressure of symbolic rivalry, for the needs of self-construction through acquisition (mostly in commodity form)'.[3]

The challenge to Christianity by commercialism is immense. Consumerism is bolstered by the power of advertising. In a global climate of 'TV viewing', the power of advertising cannot be avoided. Its role is to persuade. Billboards are everywhere – even by the slums of Kolkata there are billboards for Coca-Cola and Cadbury's chocolate. No one is immune. Children living close to or below the breadline in Britain have to face advert after advert enticing them with desirable toys and fashion as they watch children's TV, let alone adult TV. Of course, they want – but if they do not have, they risk social exclusion. Advertising leads to purchasing of the non-essential.

Shopping and advertising do not alleviate inequality. Universal happiness is promised, but it cannot deliver. What about those who neither can nor want to consume? They become isolated from full participation in social life. Society has been driven by what we want, not by what we may need, and inequalities throughout the world have been perpetuated. Much of the world continues to live in dire poverty. In Bangalore, I saw KFC, Pizza Hut, Cyber Café, Wimpy and Levi stores lining its main street, as beggars stood outside, maimed and emaciated. Not far away lay a vast slum. Values on a global scale have become me-orientated, as we live for the moment, and others becomes largely invisible. We learn to see what we can see. We channel-hop through TV and our lives.

Modern church historians have found strong links between increased leisure provision and a marked decline in churchgoing since 1945. As the critical post-war period began, increased possibilities for leisure generated a climate of choice; church gradually became just one of many options for what to do on a Sunday. Whereas less than 100 years ago the choice for many urban dwellers was the church or the pub, now there is a vast array of leisure options on Sunday. From 1851, the church took responsibility for many of the leisure activities available, as part of its evangelistic strategy (e.g. Aston Villa Football Club, which has strong church roots). However, since the First World War this public role has decreased and has become part of municipal, public structures. Contact with church in public life has therefore decreased a great deal.

Today church is not part of the experience of the vast majority of British society. Less than 1 per cent of a very diverse north London community I served in attended the local church. Today, on Sundays, church is just one option amongst many. How the church can respond to these changes remains a challenge – worship outside Sundays, Messy Church and other 'Fresh Expressions' are becoming more prevalent.

In our society, the power of the individual has been set up as the ideal for making choices; people make moral choices without any understanding of the whole notion of context, both historical and cultural. Prizing autonomy also leads to the manipulation of relationships. We see this in the constant breakdown of relationships, even amongst churchgoers. As a curate, I was astonished to see a member of my congregation on national TV proclaiming that she'd had five children, each with a different father. Moral breakdown is equally possible in society, as shown by the city riots of 2011.

Individuals or 'packs' belong to a culture where 'they feel no common truths compelling enough to bind them to the rest of society'.[4]

Debt and poverty

I recently encountered an interview with Patrick Regan, director of the youth charity XLP (the eXceL Project), a Christian charity working on twenty-two London estates and in schools whose catchment is drawn from the estates. The charity addresses issues 'such as bullying and intimidation, weapons, boredom due to a lack of organised activities, absence of parents, gangs and living in areas with high crime rates'.[5] In the interview, Mr Regan asserted that child poverty is a huge problem in Britain. He suggested that the government needs to do more to tackle the gap between rich and poor, and for political parties to talk to each other about alleviating child poverty, despite their differences. He called for the church to alleviate poverty, not only financially but by building friendships with poorer people one-on-one. He referred to a report from the Fabian society,[6] which claimed 3.6 million more people, of whom 1.2 million are children, will be living in poverty by 2030 unless the government takes 'dramatic action'. This would be an increase in child poverty of 47 per cent. The report says that cuts to welfare, and a growing gap between the amount people earn and the cost of living, are the reason for the increase in poverty. It calls for the government to create 'very high levels of employment' and also 'a high minimum wage and widespread uptake of the living wage'. The government says a record number of people are in work, and that they're cutting the budget deficit fairly, making sure the richest in society carry the heaviest burden. Kevin ran a Salvation Army youth project on a number of estates. He commented:

Child poverty is a huge issue. The young people come to our after-school drop-ins, we give them some decent food, and a lot say, 'That's all we'll get tonight'. A lot are missing toiletries; some girls cannot afford sanitary products. If there is any food left, they take loads out with them. On the face of it, they're dressed in the most amazing clothes. But we know that they'd rather look cool, look good and go hungry. Then there's the lure of drugs, of gangs, of needing to belong. Parents are struggling; blokes get into crime easily. One of our lads told me how his dad took him out on burglaries as a seven-year-old: because he was small he could get through the open bathroom windows. The mums have to hold it together because a lot of dads are absent, some in prison. They hold down two jobs and barely make ends meet. Nagging poverty makes kids angry. They go into the city and see how other people live. We give them a safe space, space to talk and good role models.

Having the right image – clothes, labels, trainers, and friends – puts enormous pressure on many parents and young people. The Children's Society report, *Who Bears the Burden: Christian Theology and the Impact of Debt on Children* ascertained that one in five families with children are living in debt, exacerbated by rising fuel bills, zero-hours contracts and changes to benefits and tax credits. The report outlines the emotional pain debt causes children:

[Debt] also damages children's relationships with their peers. More than half of children aged 10–17 in families with problem debt, said they had been embarrassed because they lacked the things that their peers had, and nearly one in five said they had been bullied as a result. In both cases, children in families with problem debt were twice as likely to suffer these problems as other children: 'I hate [school]. Because my mum and dad can't afford the trousers so I have to wear trackies. But my head of my college, I always really annoy him. He goes 'You got to get your trousers sorted out'. There is evidence that the emotional distress caused by problem debt can lead to children facing difficulty in school. Around a quarter of children in problem debt were unhappy with their life at school . . . making them nearly twice as likely as other children to be unhappy in this area of their life.[7]

The lack of money can lead people to resort to taking out payday loans, or even using illegal loan sharks who charge extortionate rates of interest – up to 3,000 per cent! The latter prey on people on council/social housing estates, and can resort to physical intimidation if people do not make payments.

Tunde had lost his job as a decorator. He and Jemima had four growing children. As the recession hit, neither could find work. When their washing machine broke down, Tunde saw a leaflet through his door about 'easy loans'. He initially borrowed £300, but then they persuaded him to borrow more. It was near Christmas, and Tunde could not accept that the children may not have decent presents. Although Jemima and the children went to church, and Tunde sometimes, they kept their debt and inner anguish secret. There is always stigma attached to debt. There is always stigma attached to not having the right image. It is a no-win situation. Tunde became trapped. For the next two years he was harassed by phone calls demanding money. The debt collectors banged on his door in the early hours of the morning and threatened to break his windows.

From one £1,000 loan he had to pay back about £1,500 but had no way to do this, so the interest kept being added on. As the loan grew to a £3,000 debt he had no way of paying, the sharks began to turn the screw. He became depressed and this affected the whole family. Jemima did eventually speak to her pastor, who referred them to a church-based debt advice centre. Tunde also borrowed from close friends and family to keep the sharks at bay. Fortunately, these sharks were tracked down but Tunde and family had to move because they felt so harassed, and in addition stigmatised on their estate. The Christian charity pointed them to credit unions, and helped them to budget. Fortunately, since 2015, the payday loans sector has been regulated, with a cap on interest rates. Councils are actively seeking out illegal loan sharks, with the intent of prosecuting them.

The Children's Society debt research found that 'children are routinely being exposed to advertising that makes high-risk, high-cost loans seem fun or normal'. In addition, almost three quarters of children aged thirteen to seventeen said they had seen at least one payday loan advert in the past seven days, one in three children said they see payday loan adverts 'all the time', and 61 per cent of parents believe that seeing payday loan adverts makes children believe these are a normal way of managing money.[8]

The Children's Society is campaigning for a ban on advertising from payday lenders before 9 p.m.:

> This irresponsible practice puts even more pressure on families struggling to make ends meet. We believe that it is not right that payday loan companies are making excessive profits on the back of exploiting children and their families, plunging them further into the debt trap. Some 74 per cent of parents agreed with us that payday loan advertisements should be banned from television and radio before the 9 p.m. watershed.

An urban church set up a debt advice centre, and soon it had huge waiting lists. People could see a trained volunteer who would help them. Advice included assessing all the paperwork, much of which seemed highly threatening, and negotiating with credit card companies and utilities providers when debts were out of control. They also helped with rigorous budgeting, which many people of all backgrounds find difficult, helping to prioritise food and basic needs. Lisa, a single mother with two young children has begun her journey to becoming debt free. However, as the project was set up to show God's love in action, Lisa was open to being prayed for in her sessions. When she came, she had no faith, but being prayed for opened up a spiritual dimension in her life. She actually joined an Alpha course.

In some cities, there is a major drive to address debt through a 'community organising'[9] initiative, to encourage people to sign up to credit unions as a way of saving, and to borrow in an ethical, regulated way, with fair interest rates. Church members in a particular area have been encouraged to sign up as a way of saving regularly, with benefits to the community, especially to prevent people from becoming prey to unregulated lenders. A credit union operates as a 'mutual' organisation and that means it is owned by its members – to save or borrow you need to be a member and live within the catchment area, often just a borough or local council. It is ethical, non-profit-making, and accessible to its community. Another church ran a three-week 'money management' course to help people budget and make good financial choices, whilst warning against the temptation of payday and illegal lenders. This course proved highly popular.

How we see ourselves

The Christian message promises a self which has been re-centred through the divine promise of hope. In an age of self-doubt and ambiguity, the gospel promises a 'hope as an anchor for the soul, firm and secure' (Hebrews 6:19). It also bestows on the self an identity of worth and purposive meaning for the present. The former is particularly important in an age of therapy, exemplified when people seek instant solutions to restore their confidence and heal their hurts. We need to alert people in sensitive ways to the fact that the Christian God has created all humanity in his own image and, as Psalm 8 reminds us, of the greatest worth. This is not to lose sight of human fallenness, but to look at the God of power and healing. Above all, the wrongly centred self can only be re-centred by being nailed to the cross. Acceptance of Christ reconfigures the self so that at the centre of the new self lies self-giving love.

The Hope Youth Project, based in a northern city, has been active for fifteen years but is now in jeopardy due to funding – it is increasingly difficult to receive 'trust' funding, on which many inner-city Christian projects are dependant. This, coupled with a climate of funding cutback, generally makes it challenging for churches to run excellent social outreach programmes. This project was born in an inner-city area because young people were vandalising the church, smoking drugs and being abusive in the church grounds. The church began to pray and seek God's will. Out of this prayer, there was a vision from the congregation members to begin a youth project – this would provide positive activities, youth drop-ins, mentoring and links to local schools. It would be open to all, and be run within the church building. There would be a Christian ethos, with the hope of engaging with the young people on Christian themes. Funding was sought, and the project had a tremendous impact on the local community – the police commented on how antisocial behaviour in the local community had been much reduced. The young people had some ownership of the building, so generally the vandalism ceased. Of course, the project had difficulties, and at times bad behaviour, but overall, it brought positive change to the lives of the young people and the community in general.

One of the key issues facing the young people was how they perceived themselves – their self-concept. Particularly during childhood and adolescence, their self-concept is enormously influenced by other people's perception of them; this is fuelled by not being able to buy into the right image, so they may find alternatives – such as deviancy, gangs, eating disorders and the quest for peer approval. Negative labelling can lead the child to behave in the way they are labelled; this is termed a 'self-fulfilling prophecy'. Being assigned to a low set in school may lead to a low self-image, reinforced by the way society treats them. Much educational research has shown that a significant number of children of Afro-Caribbean heritage fail to achieve well because they are expected to achieve badly; the prophecy becomes self-fulfilled and they become disenfranchised from education.

Although there are many exceptions, by adolescence, the peer group has also become a 'significant other', and peer groups often form a subculture in school, based on a refusal to work. The individual sees their identity not only in terms of themselves but as part of a group; peer group pressure leads to low achievement; this also forms a resistance to being labelled. Low self-image will lead to frustration, which can be translated in many ways, including deviancy. David Sheppard's observation of how a cycle of violence ensues is still relevant. Through quoting Robert Kennedy, he notes: 'The violent youth of the ghetto is not simply protesting at this condition, but making a destructive and self-defeating attempt to assert his worth and dignity as a human being, to tell us that, though we may scorn his contribution, we must still respect his power.'[10]

The Hope Youth Project works tirelessly to address issues of low self-esteem through groups and mentoring. Here is an insight of an interview with Kyle, now seventeen, a regular user of the youth project, who has grown much in self-esteem through the support, mentoring, and training he has received.

How long have you been coming to this youth project?

I have been coming for seven years. The project means a lot to me because it keeps us off the streets. It's a place to go to enjoy/have fun/ chat with friends/leaders. It's a great place to make friends.

How has the project helped you change?

The project has helped me to deal with my anger, calm down and relax more. It has given me the opportunity to go on trips and try new things. It has given me the opportunity to become a young leader and see things from a leader's point of view. I am more mature now I am a leader and it's helped me grow.

What do you like about the project?

It's great fun with lots to do. Great food (I love the hot chocolate). The leaders are funny too. My best memory is camping in the church. Waking up to bacon sandwiches and then setting off to [a theme park]. Wicked. I got to go on this trip because I finished my focus sessions on anger with full points.

How did you become a young leader yourself?

I became a young leader by passing a ten-week course on peer mentoring. On this course we acted out different situations and did written work. It was good and I enjoyed the company and the help. It's great being a young leader, it is a good experience. It's good to see how it was when we were younger from a leader's point of view. It has given me confidence in my ability get alongside other young people.

Kyle is now asking his Christian youth worker questions about faith, and has asked for a Youth Bible. The youth worker lived out his Christian faith through his actions and attitudes. Kyle's self-esteem is much healthier and he has learned to serve others, instead of always wanting or being the victim.

In the next chapter we will see how the rapid growth of the church led to a major dilemma for the apostles: practical care for the most needy or evangelising and 'being out there'. This translates into the age-old debate of evangelism or social action.

Action

- Reflect on Jesus' teaching on money (e.g. Luke 12:13–31; Matthew 6:19–34). What challenges you about your own attitude to money and material possessions?
- Now reread Acts 2:42–47 slowly, and pause. Are you challenged to change your lifestyle in any way?
- Think about your investments and savings, if applicable – can you invest more ethically? Is there a Credit Union you can save in?
- Is there an inner-city or estate youth project or youth worker you can support (prayerfully, financially, volunteering)?

Endnotes

1. William Blake, Letter to Rev John Trusler, 1777.
2. Zygmunt Bauman, *Intimations of Postmodernity* (London: Routledge, 1992), p. 49.
3. Bauman, *Intimations*, p. 50.
4. Vernon White, *Paying Attention to the People* (London: SPCK, 1996), p. 50.
5. www.xlp.org.uk (accessed 15.7.15).
6. www.fabians.org.uk/wp-content/uploads/2015/02/Inequality2030.pdf (accessed 22.1.18).

7. www.childrenssociety.org.uk/sites/default/files/tcs/debt_trap_-_theology_report. pdf (accessed 16.1.18).

8. www.childrenssociety.org.uk/the-debt-trap-end-the-damage-to-children (accessed 16.1.18).

9. Community organising is a broad-based alliance of different organisations, e.g. faiths, unions, schools, who campaign together on particular issues facing their community. I will return to this in Chapter 11.

10. David Sheppard, *Bias to the Poor* (London: Hodder & Stoughton, 1983), p. 74.

6
Called to Serve Practically

Justice is a relationship of agreement, which exists in real terms between two things whoever they are.

Montesquieu, *Les Lettres Persanes*[1]

Montesquieu, writing in the eighteenth century, in a context of Enlightenment, perceives justice as a social contract, respecting the rights of others, and not entering into a relationship where the other is harmed. Any break in the relationship is the fundamental source of all evil, resulting in dehumanisation. Montesquieu has had great influence on the legal processes of the Western world. In terms of biblical ethics, evil and the inhuman treatment of others is contrary to God's law and God's ways. This is an important theme with the Old Testament prophets, and these values underpin the life of the early church, where there was a deliberate world view which protected the poor and alienated. In Acts 6, the apostles get caught up in a conflict between the ministry of the word of God and serving at tables. In modern-day terms, this equates to the long, fraught struggle in the church over the relationship between evangelism and social action.

The apostles' dilemma: word or deed?

To begin, we will ascertain how the apostles dealt with a logistical dilemma they were faced with. The early church, from its outset, was multicultural. At this stage, the two major groups were the Hebraic Jews (which included the apostles, the church leaders) and the Hellenistic Jews. The many converts were from many different cultures, but shared Judaism as their religious heritage. The Hebraic Jews consisted of those who resided in Jerusalem, but also others who had come to Jerusalem for the Feast of Weeks and had got caught up in the wonderful move of the Spirit at Pentecost, becoming followers of Jesus. From Acts 2:9–11 we know that pilgrims included 'Parthians, Medes and Elamites;

residents of Mesopotamia, Judea and Cappadocia, Pontus and Asia, Phrygia and Pamphylia, Egypt and the parts of Libya near Cyrene; visitors from Rome (both Jews and converts to Judaism); Cretans and Arabs'. The Hellenistic Jews mentioned in 6:1 were Greek-speaking Jews who had moved to Jerusalem as part of the diaspora.

A problem is posed: the Hellenistic Jews were complaining that 'their widows were being overlooked in the daily distribution of food' (v. 1). It is likely that incoming Hellenistic Jews in Jerusalem may have been looked upon with dislike and suspicion by the indigenous Jews, who saw themselves as pure. The 'incomers' would have had different languages (Greek/native languages), values and culture. We can see from this that suspicion of and disdain for newcomers into a community is not a new phenomenon.

Distributing food must have been a highly complex operation for the apostles; the early church shared everything and there were already over 8,000 members. The widows, a group of people with no rights, depended on the support of their families – and if they had no family, or were estranged from their family, relied on benefactors for the basics of food and shelter. This is still a common issue today in many developing countries. Society was run on very patriarchal lines, and women had no rights of inheritance. Interestingly, my mother – who was born in 1929 in India, into a wealthy family – had no rights of inheritance as a daughter, something that caused her great consternation. Fortunately, the law has now changed and women do have equal rights of inheritance.

For the early Christian community it was a given that no one should be neglected, so widows were given food daily. The Torah principles of caring for the needs of the oppressed underpinned their theology, e.g. Deuteronomy 10:18: 'He defends the cause of the fatherless and the widow, and loves the foreigner residing among you, giving them food and clothing.' Clearly something had gone wrong, as the Hellenistic widows were being overlooked. To the Hellenistic Jews, it looked as though the Hebraic Jews were being favoured.

It is noteworthy that Luke does not spend much time on the inner tensions of the community, but rather is eager to emphasise the outward-looking, missional focus of the apostles.[2] The solution of the apostles can be described as 'a rather novel one for antiquity . . . Those with political power generally repressed complaining minorities; here the apostles hand the whole system over to the offended minority.'[3] Until then, it would seem that the apostles had administered the money and food, but by this time the community had grown so enormous, spending their time on this kind of service would have taken them away from the ministry of praying, preaching and evangelising.

Peter exhorted the community to select seven men to administer the food and take care of associated practical arrangements. The Greek word for waiting at tables is *diakonia*, from where we derive the ministry of deacon or diaconate. These men had to have specific gifts, and be 'full of the Spirit and wisdom' (v. 3). They selected seven men: 'Stephen, a man full of faith and of the Holy Spirit; also Philip, Procorus, Nicanor, Timon, Parmenas, and Nicolas from Antioch, a convert to Judaism' (v. 5). The group was representative and largely comprised Greek-speaking Jews and a convert (Nicolas). This is a healthy model of celebrating diversity. It is human nature to choose 'people like us', which may explain why many churches are run by educated or middle-class men, certainly in terms of leadership. Hopefully, in my own denomination, as women become bishops and more and more women are called into ministry, this will start to change. The Methodist Church has a significant number of women superintendents, and has much to teach the church as a whole in this area.

The chosen seven were presented to the apostles, 'who prayed and laid their hands on them' (v. 6). The act of laying hands to commission someone is significant – it testifies that their gifts and service are recognised as part of the work of the kingdom. As has happened many times in history, the apostles could have concentrated on preaching the word whilst ignoring human need, but the model in Acts is one of word and deed – the word is preached but no one is neglected, and certainly not the oppressed and those without traditional rights. The Romans looked down on the poor, stereotyping them as vagabonds and thieves.

The early church is radical in its thinking and is countercultural. The calling to be a deacon or overseer is not to be seen in lesser terms, but as a different ministry, reflecting the Pauline theology of the Body of Christ – that we all have different gifts and different kinds of service (1 Corinthians 12). As Paul explained to Timothy, the qualities required were to be full of the Spirit and to be people of good character and seen as trustworthy:

> In the same way, deacons are to be worthy of respect, sincere, not indulging in much wine, and not pursuing dishonest gain. They must keep hold of the deep truths of the faith with a clear conscience. They must first be tested; and then if there is nothing against them, let them serve as deacons.
>
> 1 Timothy 3:8–10

Serving as a deacon does not preclude other spiritual gifts. Stephen, one of the chosen and described as 'a man full of God's grace and power, performed great wonders and signs among the people' (6:8). In, fact his spiritual boldness led to his trial and ultimately his death.

Founded in the 1970s, the Churches Together Soup Kitchen, run by a group of local churches in a borough, is open every Saturday and Sunday, 3.30 p.m.–5 p.m. in a church hall. The Soup Kitchen serves hot food and drinks to the homeless and needy in the vicinity. The beneficiaries can also access advice and a selection of clothing and blankets. The soup kitchen has a Christian manager and volunteers from different churches, including Pentecostal, Catholic, Anglican and Baptist. The host church noticed that many beneficiaries were staying on after the soup kitchen for the informal café service. In fact, after a few months, they were the majority of the congregation, so the church reflectively changed its communication style to more discussion-based rather than traditional sermons.

The soup kitchen has developed into an ecumenical vision of providing accommodation in the colder months. Each night a different church accommodates up to twenty homeless men and women, allowing them to sleep in warmth and providing breakfast. Although the project does not seek to proselytise, on different occasions, beneficiaries ask for prayer. Often, having suffered traumas in their lives, such as domestic abuse, violence, drug abuse, they feel able to open up to the Christian volunteers who pray for healing for them. Sam had come in, in desperation. He had not been able to sleep due to a sore on his leg and had started shouting and swearing in the night. Two volunteers came to him and quietly offered to pray for him, in the vestibule where it was more private. They laid hands over him, and immediately Sam felt peace and a sense of the Holy Spirit. He slept well that night and told his friends what had happened in the morning. Through practical service, different gifts come into play. Gifts are not mutually exclusive, as we learn from Stephen.

A great divorce - evangelism and social action

In the modern world, somehow social action and evangelism became separated. By 1875, the vast majority of evangelicals were seeking to withdraw from the world into a 'deeper-life' spirituality. The Keswick movement was born and 8,000 evangelicals met together to affirm the 'holiness movement'. The holiness movement was suspicious of Christians involved in social action and instead emphasised the individual's conversion and believing in a 'second work of grace', in which Christians are 'sanctified' so that they may be free from sin. This experience of sanctification enables the believer to live a holy life. Following this doctrine placed great emphasis on personal salvation and the individual's spiritual journey. From fear of contamination, there was a tendency to withdraw from social issues. This explains, at least in part, why the evangelical and later the evangelical charismatic movement was so strong in wealthy or suburban areas, and much less visible in the inner cities. In the Church of England, the predominant church at that time, it was the Anglo-Catholics who were the pioneers in the slums and degradation of the inner cities. F.D. Maurice is associated with 'Christian Socialism', which advocated 'a rejection of evangelical categories of sin and personal salvation'.[4]

A great polarisation between evangelicals and liberal Catholics began, and the evangelicals largely kept away from social action, from fear of liberal theology. There were notable exceptions: the Baptist minister F.B. Meyer attempted to hold together mission (in his view, conversion) with social action. He had come face-to-face with terrible poverty in London and Leicester. He preached against drunkenness and prostitution. He is said to have brought about the closing of hundreds of saloons and brothels – 700 to 800 between 1885 and 1907. He combined evangelism with social action, generally seeing drink as the root of society's ills, but did not shy away from desiring that the mass of people 'hail the religion of Jesus Christ'. Meyer interpreted Jesus' own commission as the Holy Spirit's anointing, 'not simply to preach the gospel of the poor, but to heal the broken-hearted by removing the causes of heartbreak; to proclaim liberty to the captive of the sweaters' den'.[5]

Around the same time, William Booth[6] published *In Darkest England and the Way Out* (1890). Although the concept of 'darkest England' being compared to 'darkest Africa' is shockingly un-PC today, his premise that Christians need to be involved in the eradication of poverty are most certainly valid. He proposed to apply the Christian gospel and work ethic to the social problems he encountered. The book speaks of abolishing vice and poverty by establishing homes for the homeless, farm communities where the urban poor could be trained in agriculture, homes for fallen women and released prisoners, aid for the poor and help for alcoholics. He said that if the state failed to meet its social obligations, it would be the task of each Christian to step into the breach. However, Booth was not departing from his spiritual convictions to set up a socialist or communist society; Booth's ultimate aim was to get people 'saved'. Booth says in his introduction:

I have no intention to depart in the smallest degree from the main principles on which I have acted in the past. My only hope for the permanent deliverance of mankind from misery, either in this world or the next, is the regeneration or remaking of the individual by the power of the Holy Ghost through Jesus Christ. But in providing for the relief of temporal misery I reckon that I am only making it easy where it is now difficult, and possible where it is now all but impossible, for men and women to find their way to the Cross of our Lord Jesus Christ.[7]

Yet, despite these radical Christian thinkers, evangelicals remained suspicious of social action. A turning point was the Lausanne Covenant in 1974, paragraph 5:

CHRISTIAN SOCIAL RESPONSIBILITY
We affirm that God is both the Creator and the Judge of all people. We therefore should share his concern for justice and reconciliation throughout human society and for the liberation of men and women from every kind of oppression. Because men and women are made in the image of God, every person, regardless of race, religion, colour, culture, class, sex or age, has an intrinsic dignity because of which he or she should be respected and served, not exploited. Here too we express penitence both for our neglect and for having sometimes regarded evangelism and social concern as mutually exclusive. Although reconciliation with other people is not reconciliation with God, nor is social action evangelism, nor is political liberation salvation, nevertheless we affirm that evangelism and socio-political involvement are both part of our Christian duty. For both are necessary expressions of our doctrines of God and man, our love for our neighbour and our obedience to Jesus Christ. The message of salvation implies also a message of judgment upon every form of alienation, oppression and discrimination, and we should not be afraid to denounce evil and injustice wherever they exist. When people receive Christ they are born again into his kingdom and must seek not only to exhibit but also to spread its

righteousness in the midst of an unrighteous world. The salvation we claim should be transforming us in the totality of our personal and social responsibilities. Faith without works is dead.[8]

This covenant, including a renewed emphasis on social action along with evangelism, gained great respect in the evangelical world. This was much helped by the fact that one of its principal architects was John Stott. Stott himself wrote of his own change in thinking by reflecting on the 'Great Commission': 'I see more clearly that not only the consequences of the commission but the actual commission itself must be understood to include social as well as evangelistic responsibility, unless we are guilty of distorting the words of Jesus.'[9]

Addressing the dichotomy of evangelism and social action, David Bosch reminds us that the mission of God is holistic, and includes both evangelism and social action. He warns against separating these results into 'two separate components':

The moment one regards mission as consisting of two separate components one has, in principle, conceded that each of the two has a life of its own. One is then by implication saying that it is possible to have evangelism with a social dimension and a Christian social involvement without an evangelistic dimension. What is more, if one suggests that one component is primary and the other secondary, one implies that the one is essential, the other optional.[10]

The hierarchies of the past, placing evangelism at the pinnacle, the highest and most revered zeal of practising Christians, has been replaced by a more integral approach to mission.[11]

When confronted by injustice, what is our Christian response? Bosch comments on his own native South Africa (sadly, he died three years before the end of apartheid):

In the context of the apartheid system and the experience of repression and police brutality during a state of emergency, evangelicals . . . had no doubt that they were called to a ministry of proclaiming Christ as Savior . . . but they were equally convinced that sin was both personal and structural, that life was of a piece, that dualism was contrary to the gospel.[12]

For Bosch, this marks an important shift in evangelicalism, as Christians need 'both personal renewal by God's Spirit *and* resolute commitment to challenging and transforming the structures of society'.[13] He expounds mission as God's mission, *missio dei*. This is a Trinitarian interpretation of mission: mission is not the work of the church but 'it is the mission of the Son and the Spirit though the Father that includes the church'.[14] Mission therefore becomes a 'movement of God into the world and the church is viewed as an instrument for that mission'. We tap into God's love, which is poured out into the world. Within this view of mission, it is the role of the Spirit to move over the world, bringing about repentance and forgiveness, bringing people to a love of Christ, and for the church to be empowered to go out to do God's work.

Evangelism *and* social action

For us today, what is the relationship between what we may perceive as 'social action' and evangelism? For years, driven by a fear of liberalism and the liberal agenda, evangelical and charismatic Christians concentrated on the need for salvation, the individual being converted to Christ through repentance and acceptance. This can be traced back to Luther's doctrine of justification by faith – 'without his witness ours is futile. Conviction of sin, faith in Christ, new birth and Christian growth are all his work.'[15]

I come from a standpoint of an evangelical, charismatic Christian, but I cannot find a biblical mandate to separate evangelism and social action. Recently, the term 'integral mission' has been coined to counteract traditional polarisation of word and deed:

Integral mission . . . is the proclamation and demonstration of the gospel . . . Justice and justification by faith, worship and political action, the spiritual and the material, personal change and structural change belong together. As in the life of Jesus, being, doing and saying are at the heart of our integral task.[16]

This moves beyond the Lausanne Covenant because evangelism and social concern are not just 'part of our Christian duty' – they are inextricably linked, there is no polarisation, they are integral to who Christians are. Integral mission also challenges us to look to Jesus himself as our model, as 'being, doing and saying' are at the heart of who he is, and therefore becomes our inspiration.

I spent a year as a missionary teacher in India. There I observed that all Christians, regardless of denomination – Catholic, evangelical and Pentecostal – were all involved in social transformation in some form. The poverty and suffering around them was so great that it would be unimaginable not to respond to the huge need before them in every community. Without showing compassion in practical ways, how could they begin to expect people to come to Jesus? To reflect Jesus' own teaching:

'For I was hungry and you gave me something to eat, I was thirsty and you gave me something to drink, I was a stranger and you invited me in, I needed clothes and you clothed me, I was ill and you looked after me, I was in prison and you came to visit me.' Then the righteous will answer him, 'Lord, when did we see you hungry and feed you, or thirsty and give you something to drink? When did we see you a stranger and invite you in, or needing clothes and clothe you? When did we see you ill or in prison and go to visit you?' The King will reply, 'Truly I tell you, whatever you did for one of the least of these brothers and sisters of mine, you did for me.'

Matthew 25:35–40

The Bethsaida Project has been running in a rural South India for thirty years. Pastor Malachi and his wife felt called there by the Holy Spirit: called to show people living in poverty and fatalism (believing that things cannot change or get better) that Jesus can transform lives and communities. They did not begin by building a church and expecting people to come to it – they were mostly people from a Dalit Hindu background, treated as untouchable, excluded and not allowed to mix, e.g. not allowed to share taps. In fact, it is a situation not dissimilar to the plight of Samaritans in Jesus' day. If they had tried to preach publicly, they would have incurred the wrath and even violence of the Hindu leaders in the community. Instead, they had to begin by building trust, reflecting Jesus' love and compassion. After prayer, they knew there were many orphans. Again, similarly to Jesus' time, orphans had no rights and no financial support. They relied on their extended families, but if their families had almost nothing already, then how could they house and feed another mouth? Orphans, five, six and seven-year-olds up to teenagers, were often forced to beg, to go into the cities to find work, and to be at the mercy of slave gangs. Malachi and his English wife, Deborah, began to take in orphans in their own home, to offer them love, care and protection. They showed Jesus' love through seeing the children as being made in the image of God, and each day they prayed with the children and shared Bible stories. Gradually they received funding from friends, initially to build an orphanage – two houses, one for girls and one for boys. A Christian ethos in every area was instilled.

The next stage of prayer and seeking God led them to start a school, open to the whole community. Seeing from the orphans that government schools provided a poor standard of education, a school was built: initially a couple of classrooms in a makeshift building with a straw roof. Deborah began the teaching and oversight of the school herself. The school was to be 'English medium', as English medium had been the domain of the wealthy, and the ability to speak English would provide a way to progress in Indian society. In a vast country of 400 languages, English still remains the common factor, even after seventy years of independence. The school became very popular in the local community.

On Sundays, Malachi began a Tamil worshipping community in the school, for the orphans. People started coming from the community. Some were Christians; others encountered the love of Jesus, or received healing through the power of the Spirit. Some faced opposition, as did Malachi from some sectors of the community, but they persevered, and the work of God is going from strength to strength in that community.

Aziz's story

In this testimony, we learn from Aziz how the love shown by a Christian project for asylum seekers and refugees became instrumental in him finding a living faith in Jesus:

I was born into a poor Muslim family. As I grew up, I developed an interest in literature, art and politics, and I read a lot and began to think in a different way. I became disturbed by the suffering around me and I felt bad about the injustice and lack of freedom in my country, Iran.

Whilst still living in Iran, I often heard speeches about freedom and justice on the radio. I eventually crossed the border to Iraq and I joined a resistance group. The leader tried to show everyone a modern and gentle side to Islam. It sounded reasonable to me and I accepted this version of Islam. But there was a lot of pressure from the rules in this group, and there was no democracy and freedom. When the American army captured Iraq in 2003, they protected our group. This was a good opportunity for those of us who wanted to escape. One night, I escaped to the American army camp, just as some of my friends had done the night before.

The Americans made a camp for us and provided us with everything we needed to live, such as food, clothes and a chance to work. They also provided us with satellite TV, which had a great influence on my life. For the first time I was able to appreciate new ideas, opinions and a different way of life. For the first time in twelve years, I was able to contact my family and I found out that my younger brother had been executed for contacting my resistance group.

During these four years in the American camp, we were given a Bible in the Farsi language. I sometimes read the gospels of the New Testament and I was attracted to the simple life and gentle character of Jesus. I was very moved by the story of Jesus stopping a woman from being stoned to death. Jesus said, 'Forgive everyone, even your enemy.'

Eventually the Americans gave us a card from the UNHCR and a travel document. I left this camp in 2008 and went to Baghdad to search for a way to leave Iraq. I went to live in a hotel, but after two months I was arrested by the Iraqi police and sent to prison because I didn't have a proper passport. After that, I managed to escape to England.

When I came to England, in those first days I looked for a church in my area and I found an Iranian Christian church nearby. In early May 2009, I started going to the meetings. At that time, I had no inclination to use my new-found interest in Christianity as a case for asylum in Britain. I was confident that my case was already secure because I had been a member of the resistance for twelve years and also because my younger brother had been executed. I never thought that the Home Office would refuse me. I now have status, but it was stressful and took a long time.

I was moved to the north of England. I went to my first Christian meeting and I listened to the words about love, kindness and beauty. I felt calm and, more than ever, felt interested in Christianity. After a while, I met one man and one woman in the street and they said that they were true Christians. They were Jehovah's Witnesses. For a few months I went to their meetings and studied their book with them. But after a while, I realised that they were wrong. They didn't believe in celebrating Christmas or the birthdays of their own children, but in the Bible Jesus encouraged people to celebrate and be happy.

I moved to [a new city] in October 2009 and I found out about a church there which had an organisation for refugees and asylum seekers. I went there and talked to the pastor, whose kindness and gentle nature was a positive influence on me, and he guided me away from the Jehovah's Witness group. I became a member of this church and accepted Jesus' forgiveness on the cross. After seven or eight months, I was baptised; I was born again and began my new life.

The first week after I was baptised I told my family. My father was annoyed and said that I had brought shame on the family. My uncles and my cousin threatened me. But it is more important for me to find the truth. I want to tell everyone about the love and kindness of Jesus. I am proud that I am a Christian.

Aziz's powerful and moving testimony tells us a great deal about the indivisible relationship between social action and evangelism. Through the project, he encountered Christian love and acceptance, and simultaneously the Holy Spirit was working in his life to bring him to the point where he was able to become a committed Christian, transformed by the forgiveness and compassion of Jesus.

In the next chapter we will follow one of the new deacons, Stephen, who found himself in a spiritual battle with the Sanhedrin. His prophetic discourse will enable deliberation on the meaning of prophecy today.

Action
- Reflect on Acts 6:1–7. What does this say to you for today?
- What is your response to the great divorce of evangelism and social action?
- What do you think discourages social action? Or evangelism?
- Look out for examples of churches engaging with social action – does this help or hinder church growth?
- Is there any way your church could grow through a specific outreach?

Endnotes
1. Montesquieu 'Les Lettres Persanes', lettre 83. Author's own translation.
2. R.C. Tannehill, *The Narrative Unity of Luke–Acts: A Literary Interpretation*

(Minneapolis, MN:FortressPress, 1990), p. 80.

3. Ben Witherington III, *The Acts of the Apostles, a Socio-Rhetorical Commentary* (Grand Rapids, MI: Williams B. Eerdmans, 1998), p. 248.

4. I. Randall in John Wolffe, ed., *Evangelical Faith and Public Zeal: Evangelicals and Society 1780–1980* (London: SPCK, 1995) p. 155.

5. Randall in Wolffe, *Evangelical Faith,* ref. 3, p. 160.

6. William and Catherine Booth started the Salvation Army in 1865.

7. General Booth, *In Darkest England and the Way Out* (London: Salvation Army, 1890).

8. www.lausanne.org/content/covenant/lausanne-covenant (accessed 15 July 2015).

9. John Stott, *Christian Mission in the Modern World* (Coventry: CPAS, 1975), p. 23.

10. David J. Bosch, *Transforming Mission* (New York: Orbis, 1991), p. 405.

11. See, for example, 'The 5 Marks of Mission' (Anglican Consultative Council, 1984–1990).

12. Bosch, *Transforming,* ref. 6, p. 407.

13. Bosch, *Transforming,* ref. 6, p. 408.

14. Bosch, *Transforming,* p. 390, quoting Moltmann.

15. *Lausanne Covenant,* para. 14.

16. *Micah Network Declaration on Integral Mission,* 2001.

7
What Does it Mean to Be Prophetic?

I have a dream that one day every valley shall be exalted, and
every hill and mountain shall be made low, the rough places will
be made plain, and the crooked places will be made straight, and
the glory of the Lord shall be revealed and all flesh shall see it
together.

Martin Luther King[1]

Martin Luther King, the Baptist-preacher-turned-civil-rights-cam-
paigner may be seen as a modern-day prophet. His speech is steeped
in Old Testament imagery and quotations. He drew on the prophetic
tradition of Jeremiah, Amos and Isaiah, who had condemned the people of Israel for their sinful ways and called upon them to repent and
return to their covenant with God. King prophesied against the sins
of racism in contemporary America, invoking a return to prophetic
tradition in which God would bless the nation if it would heed the call
of the Old Testament prophets to 'act justly and to love mercy and to
walk humbly with your God' (Micah 6:8). Like the Hebrew prophets,
King saw no clear distinction between the sacred world of the Holy
Spirit and the secular world of corrupt society. Quoting Amos 5:24,
King said, 'We will not be satisfied until justice rolls down like waters
and righteousness like a mighty stream.'[2] Then in words based on the
passion of Jesus on the cross, he urged those who had been 'battered
by the storms of persecution and staggered by the winds of police brutality' to stand firm in 'the faith that unearned suffering is redemptive.'[3]

In this chapter we will look at whether there is any place for prophecy,
in the tradition of the Old Testament prophets, today. What are the
issues we need to stand up and speak out about? Should we defend
the rights of the poor and the downtrodden? Stephen is an example of
someone martyred for his faith. He spoke out against his persecutors

in prophetic fashion. We will explore different understandings of Old Testament and New Testament prophecy, asking whether these are mutually exclusive, or whether we heed both.

Stephen – a voice calling in the wilderness

Acts 6:8 to Acts 8:1 builds up to and culminates in the martyrdom of Stephen, the first of the Christian leaders to be executed for his Christian faith. The acts of performing miracles and proclaiming the reign of Jesus had upset the authorities and the Sanhedrin. Luke gives this incident a considerable amount of attention, dwelling predominantly on Stephen's prophetic boldness in face of antagonism from the Sanhedrin.

Stephen was arrested because he 'performed great wonders and signs among the people' (6:8). Luke emphasises that Stephen was full of the Holy Spirit. It is the power of the Holy Spirit that enabled Stephen to perform the great wonders and signs (we are not told exactly what these were, but probably they included healings and individuals turning to Christ). Stephen was 'full of God's grace and power' (6:8), filled with, and buoyed up by, the Holy Spirit – nothing was going to hinder him in performing God's work, not even oppressive, menacing opposition. When the Jews began to argue with him, 'they could not stand up against the wisdom the Spirit gave him as he spoke' (6:10). It was the Holy Spirit who gave him the words to proclaim truth, and Luke accentuates the Spirit's supernatural power. As Witherington observes:

> We are meant to hear an echo of Jesus' promise found in Luke 21:15 – 'for I will give you a mouth and wisdom that none of your opponents will be able to withstand or contradict.' Stephen's life not merely parallels Jesus', but we see in him the fulfillment of what Jesus promised his disciples he would equip them with for their witness.[4]

In the next scene, finding themselves unable to suppress the work of the Holy Spirit, the members of the synagogue fabricated false evidence against Stephen, namely that he had spoken blasphemous words against Moses and against God. As a result, Stephen was brought in front of the Sanhedrin, surrounded by false witnesses who intimated that Stephen claimed that the synagogue would be destroyed by Jesus. It is interesting to note that they were attached to the physical nature of their holy place, whereas the apostles were very much led to wherever the Spirit called them.

I am reminded of people who refer to 'my church', common on outer estate churches, and see the church as a building which they cling onto, even in the face of rapidly dwindling numbers. The New Testament vision of church was very much about going out into all the world, being led by the Spirit and proclaiming Jesus at every opportunity. Tannehill observes:

> Stephen warns against any implied restriction of God to the temple. With the assistance of Isaiah 66:1–2 he proclaims the transcendence of God. God is not dependent on works of human hands, nor do temples of human construction define God's location or 'place of rest'; humans do not make things for God as if God were in need of anything.[5]

So, the work of God through the Holy Spirit and proclaimed in Jesus' name is beyond human limitations of time and place; it is the work, leading and the power of the Godhead that is paramount.

This led, of course, to Stephen being vilified by the religious elite – those whose religious traditions and sacred places had been called into question. Luke portrays Stephen as a prophet, in the sense of the Old Testament prophets – he was undeniably fearless in face of human opposition, he spoke out God's inspired words boldly, and challenged the false religion and hypocrisy of the complacent. For example, Stephen compared himself to the prophets, who in their time had been rejected by their auditors: 'Was there ever a prophet your ancestors did not persecute?' (7:52) and quoted from the prophets Amos and Isaiah. From Amos, he had previously alluded to the practice of bringing insincere, meaningless worship to God, combined with worship to idols. God himself rejected their worship: 'Did you bring me sacrifices and offerings for forty years in the wilderness, people of Israel? You have taken up the tabernacle of Molek and the star of your god Rephan, the idols you made to worship' (7:42–43). Stephen emphasised that their insincerity led to the exile of the Israelites, who had failed in their calling be God's chosen people, offered up insincere worship and neglected the poor.

This all built up to the pinnacle of Stephen's prophetic tirade: the death of Jesus. Stephen focused blame on the chief priests and their associates for Jesus' death: 'You stiff-necked people! Your hearts and ears are still uncircumcised. You are just like your ancestors: you always resist the Holy Spirit!' (Acts 7:51). Stephen then criticised the adherence of the Sanhedrin, the chief priests and the elders, to legalism: their adherence to circumcision as a ritual that was divorced from their actual behaviours. His strong indictment, 'And now you have betrayed and murdered him – you who have received the law that was given through angels but have not obeyed it' (Acts 7:52–53) clearly laid blame for the death of Jesus at the feet of the Sanhedrin.

In Luke's eyes, Stephen was vindicated of all the charges, even though his earthly life would end. Like Jesus, he had been tried falsely and executed but, as in the resurrection, the righteousness of God triumphed over evil. Stoned to death for alleged blasphemy, 'Stephen, full of the Holy Spirit, looked up to heaven and saw the glory of God, and Jesus standing at the right hand of God. "Look," he said, "I see heaven open and the Son of Man standing at the right hand of God"' (7:55–56). At the point of death, he handed himself over to Jesus: 'Lord Jesus, receive my spirit' (7:59), then implored God to forgive his executioners, reminiscent of Jesus' words, unique to Luke: 'Father, forgive them, for they do not know what they are doing' (Luke 23:34). He then fell asleep, dying peacefully in face of terrible brutality, demonstrating the power of love in the face of human self-delusion and sinfulness.

Stephen is portrayed as a prophet who annunciates the words of God, pointing people back to God's covenant, this time the new covenant, built on Jesus Christ. In the style of the Old Testament prophets, he denounced the evil ways of the religious people of the day, for not keeping God's covenant, and rejecting God's truths.

Prophecy today

In charismatic circles, prophecy is generally understood as announcing the words received by an individual church by means of the Holy Spirit's power. The root of this understanding can be found in Paul's much-quoted first letter to the Corinthians, where prophecy is depicted as one of the spiritual gifts, for the purpose of building up the church. In 1 Corinthians 14:3, Paul states: 'But the one who prophesies speaks to people for their strengthening, encouraging and comfort.' The purpose of prophecy is to edify the church: for the church to listen to God, seek fresh vision from him and to move in the direction he is calling them. This kind of prophecy has a place in the church today.

In a relatively small and materially poor church of which I was minister, prophecy had played a strong part in encouraging the church faithful to look to God and his purposes. In its thirty-year history, a significant prophecy received was in its very nature biblical – Jeremiah 29:11, '"For I know the plans I have for you," declares the LORD, "plans to prosper you and not to harm you, plans to give you hope and a future."' This prophecy was often called upon as a reminder of God's faithfulness; the church were encouraged by this assurance of God's plans, protection and guidance, as they could have felt vulnerable. They were a congregation of about thirty, in a very small 1970s building which the council had their eye on, surrounded by vast council buildings and blocks of maisonettes; they could easily have felt dwarfed and insignificant. Furthermore, Christians were a minority – the area was around 75 per cent other faiths, mostly Sikh and Muslim. The prophecy became truth through some significant occurrences, usually around financial struggles, which was a key issue to this congregation. On a number of occasions, when there was an appeal for finance, the exact amount of money came in – to the penny. Sometimes these were small, for example to buy new heaters, and sometimes significant, such as to employ a youth worker. In my time, one Monday evening at the church council, the council proposed we raise money for a data projector/laptop and loop system, with the aim of being more accessible in our worship. The meeting ended at 9 p.m. About 9.30 p.m. I went to read my emails and found there was a message from a neighbouring church explaining that they had felt called to give £400 to our church. Miraculously, this would pay for our own new technology. This all testifies to the fulfilment of the prophecy as great spiritual encouragement to the church community, with the faith of fringe members also strengthened.

Another prophecy was that the church should be the heartbeat of the community. Here was an estate church, now with a youth and community worker. This was the era of Neighbourhood Renewal and the church became very high profile within the local community. In terms of initiatives, any new initiative on the estate came to the minister and community worker first. Social capital was able to be built up, as the church built bridges with different community groups, and the profile of the church increased significantly. In addition, the church was seen as the main and most reliable provider of youth work, as council initiatives and workers came and went.

There is definitely a place for prophecy to build up the church. The examples above are not of suburban – large, charismatic – churches, but struggling churches, ministering in deprived communities, actually building up the resources of that community. In the same letter, Paul talks about the gift of tongues, which is used for edifying the self: 'Anyone who speaks in a tongue edifies themselves, but the one who prophesies edifies the church' (1 Corinthians 14:4). In our individualistic culture, sadly sometimes prophecy has become a gift to edify the individual, and not the church. An altar call after the sermon may pertain to something going on in the life of individuals – which of course is prerequisite – but how does this impact the life of the church as a corporate body? Naturally, we all need building up in faith, but we are all part of one body and the purpose of the gifts is to edify the whole; to be built together to be a 'holy temple' (Ephesians 2:21). I am advocating an outward-looking focus, onto what Paul calls the 'common good'.

Prophecy: challenging injustice

What part is played by the Old Testament understanding of prophecy, in bringing people back to God's ways and proclaiming God's desire for justice? Does this have a place today? This aspect of prophecy has become all but lost, certainly in evangelical/charismatic circles. The prophet Amos prophesied during the reign of King Jeroboam I (786–746 BC), ruler of the northern kingdom of Israel, which was enjoying a time of unrivalled prosperity in the history of Israel, but equally a period of extreme moral and social disintegration. It was during this period that Amos began to prophesy. Amos was called by God to speak out against injustice and ungodliness, guided by the Holy Spirit. Israel's sins were self-inflicted. Judah had not kept God's law (2:4) and Israel was exploiting the poor and lacked morals (2:6–7). Amos' prophecy was based on the extent to which the covenant Yahweh made with his chosen people was being ignored in Israel. Amos states: 'Hear this word, people of Israel, the word the LORD has spoken against you – against the whole family I brought up out of Egypt: "You only have I chosen of all the families of the earth; therefore I will punish you for all your sins"' (Amos 3:1–2).

Ignoring the covenant relationship with Yahweh had led to two major forms of sin: social sin and religious sin, both integral to understanding covenant law, and therefore linked. Israel's society was strongly divided into two. The wealthy property-owning class lived by exploiting the poor. Amos is directly addressing Israel's ruling class, where the rich lived in luxury. He condemns them for their indulgent and complacent lifestyle: reclining, feasting, listening to music and imbibing rather too much wine (Amos 6). Amos condemns this lifestyle, as it is based on exploiting the poor: the justice system was run by this property-owning class, and slaves, widows and orphans had no one to stand up for them. Bribery was commonplace and business practices were fraudulent ('cheating with dishonest scales', 8:5).

The second kind of sin was religious sin. Despite ignoring much of the law by committing social sin, there was much religious activity going on, but it was highly insincere. This form of cultic worship also goes back to the Pentateuch, where social justice is also demanded. God condemned Israel, refusing their sacrifices and worship, because they disregarded the covenant. Amos warns that it is the rich, living in luxury, who will be condemned to exile first (6:7). Yahweh has sworn that he desires sincere worship, but above all he desires his people to return to him and follow his laws. As a result, Amos' message is one of complete destruction for Israel. Amos speaks in a series of visions, which he says have been shown to him by God, to describe the end of Israel (chs 7–8). The plumb line (7:7–9) is of particular significance: this is the measure of being in a balanced, healthy relationship with God, which can only occur if God's people act justly and sincerely follow God's law.

Asylum seekers and refugees: an example of prophecy today

Like Stephen, who addressed the evils and injustices of the religious leaders and elite, the church needs to find again a prophetic voice to challenge society's injustices and dehumanising practices. The world of Amos is not dissimilar to our world today. As Amos, we are often called to challenge government policies, both local and national.

We will look at the example of asylum seekers and refugees to illustrate injustice today. In one church, there is a particular ministry to asylum seekers and refugees who find themselves moved to such areas and then feel isolated. A number wander into their local church looking for spiritual resources and emotional support in the face of considerable hardship.

Benji fled Iran. He became interested in Christianity through a school friend who was secretive about his faith, but Benji, then aged seventeen, saw that his friend had an inner peace and that there was something 'very different about him'. In a supernatural experience of

Jesus, he converted to Christianity and started going to an underground church with his friend. He was aware of the dangers of converting and worshipping Jesus in a church setting, but his love of Jesus was so great that he could not resist the Spirit's power. One day, he discovered that his pastor had been arrested, and the 'moral police' were looking for all the members of that church. His mother had had a visit from the police, and had warned Benji. Benji hid in a friend's garden for two days, while his family arranged to pay for his escape from Iran. For two weeks, he was hidden in a lorry – an experience he described to me – which was horrific beyond description. For fear of his life, he was trapped with other people, at the mercy of people traffickers.

Once he reached the UK, he was dumped in the middle of nowhere and told to find his way to the nearest police station. Immediately he was detained, his story was not thought credible and the dangers he faced if deported were not considered valid. He was first moved to an asylum centre, where a Christian project was working, and from there moved to a shared flat in a neighbouring area. Here he began attending church regularly and growing in faith. His claim for asylum was rejected at first, but on appeal, after a fresh claim, he was granted leave to remain. Members of the church supported him emotionally, in prayer and financially. I have met many people like Benji, some women and many men. Even with a solicitor, many cases are rejected.

Anthony Harvey comments:

Typically, an asylum seeker who arrives at a British port or airport has left his or her own country to escape death or torture, has had to make a secret departure either with no travel documents or with false ones provided by smugglers or traffickers, has lost contact with family and friends, has made a difficult and dangerous journey across continents, and is then confronted (often in a strange language) by stringent bureaucratic regulations that have to be understood and complied with in a matter of days if the claim for asylum is to have any hope of success.[6]

The majority of cases do not have positive outcomes, and the asylum seekers are left caught in a seemingly eternal, horrific, Kafkaesque bureaucratic nightmare. Benji goes to 'sign' every two weeks; each time he is in fear of being arrested and deported, as many of his friends have been arrested and taken into detention.

Asylum has become a hot political topic. There are many myths around asylum seekers and refugees, and people often do not realise the dangers they have faced in their home countries. According to a MORI poll, British people believe that the UK has 23 per cent of the world's refugees, whereas in fact the UK houses 2 per cent of the world's refugees – two thirds of the world's refugees live in developing countries and in 2008 the UK ranked seventeenth in the league table of industrialised countries for the number of applications for asylum per head of population.[7]

Another myth is that asylum seekers are 'illegal'. Again this is not the case, as in 1951 the UK signed the Convention on Refugees giving anyone the right to seek asylum until a final decision has been made on their application. Furthermore, I will try to dispel the misconception that asylum seekers abuse the welfare system and receive large benefits. In fact, a single person currently receives only £35.52 (per week), which is 30 per cent below the poverty line. A very small percentage of asylum seekers may be involved in crime, and the press picks up on this, suggesting that most asylum seekers are part of criminal gangs. Recently the emphasis has turned to Eastern Europeans, who are lumped together into one bracket, often as criminals or alcoholics.

Being prophetic means that as Christians we need to stand up, campaign and speak out on behalf of those who are being oppressed. There is a strong biblical mandate for including 'the outsiders', those who are excluded because of government policy and human prejudice.

Nick Spencer explores the biblical mandate for the proper Christian care and hospitality towards those seeking asylum.[8] The Hebrew Bible refers to the *ger* (plural *gerim*).

Ger is usually translated 'alien' or 'sojourner' but is a more subtle term than either of those terms suggest. Throughout the Old Testament, *gerim* are often mentioned alongside hired hands, the poor, widows and orphans, implying they were dependent, vulnerable members of society. Although the Jubilee legislation in Leviticus chapter 25 makes it clear that *gerim* could acquire economic stability and power, in the main the law acknowledges that they were vulnerable people and needed support in much the same way as those Israelites who had fallen out of their normal social network. In this respect, the *ger* had much in common with the asylum applicant.[9]

In a similar vein to the widows and orphans we encountered in Acts 6, the *gerim* are the vulnerable, in need of godly support. In Leviticus, the law stated that: 'When a foreigner [*ger*] resides among you in your land, do not ill-treat them. The foreigner residing among you must be treated as your native-born. Love them as yourself, for you were foreigners in Egypt' (Lev. 19:33–34). It is fascinating to note that God reminds the Israelites that an essential event in their history is the Exodus – that God effected their flight from slavery.

The prophet Ezekiel admonishes Jerusalem, around the time of the exile, for its mistreatment of the *ger* (aliens), the fatherless and widows – in short, those with few rights. 'See how each of the princes of Israel who are in you uses his power to shed blood . . . in you they have oppressed the foreigner and ill-treated the fatherless and the widow' (Ezekiel 22:6–7).

Jesus himself, when questioned about which of the commandments is the most important, summed up the law as: '"Love the Lord your God with all your heart and with all your soul and with all your mind." This is the first and greatest commandment. And the second is like it: "Love your neighbour as yourself." All the Law and the Prophets hang on these two commandments' (Matthew 22:37–40).

The fundamental question is, how do we treat our neighbour, particularly the alien and the oppressed? Living this out is fundamental to Luke's theology. I make numerous references to the Samaritans. In the well-known parable of the Good Samaritan, 'the hero of Christ's parable was not only an alien but a despised alien. The call to transcend national loyalties when faced with those in need could not have been made more provocatively'.[10]

Farida had been educated to graduate level and had worked as an accountant in Sierra Leone, but escaped during the civil war, after one of her sons was captured and made to fight by the guerrillas. Finding herself in Britain after such trauma, she found her qualifications had no value. With a strained back, caused by hiding under a bed for week, she worked at a branch of a national chain of chemists, standing on her feet eight hours a day, at great discomfort to herself. It is painful that people escaping trauma feel devalued and dehumanised. The daughter of an Eritrean friend is a neurologist, but living in Italy, all she is able to do is work as a waitress. This seems such a waste of someone's talent and vocation, especially as often there are chronic shortages in the health professions. In the UK, asylum seekers are not allowed to work, even though the majority would like to contribute positively to the host's economy. Incidences of mental illness amongst asylum seekers are extremely high. As prophets, we are surely called to question a system which degrades people and causes them illness.

In terms of a prophetic response, faced with huge numbers of destitute asylum seekers, Harvey comments:

> For a Christian, as for so many of other faiths or none, what is being done to them in our name represents nothing less than a scandalous affront to the dignity of our fellow human beings and a denial of some of our most basic instincts of compassion and solidarity. That they should be assured of their basic human rights to the minimum of sustenance, shelter and freedom of movement must be a high priority in any society which claims to live by Christian values.[11]

An organisation with Christian roots in community organising –

and supported actively by different churches and faiths – is London Citizens. They have campaigned on behalf of the 300,000 to 500,000 'illegals' that have outstayed their welcome but now exist by working in the underground economy. The campaign 'Strangers into Citizens' seeks to 'facilitate action by ordinary citizens to achieve goals . . . which are strongly desired by many but which the government fails to promote'.[12] This campaign is to grant British citizenship to such people after four years – in effect, an amnesty. This policy has been rejected by the government on the grounds that such a policy would only encourage more immigration.

A number of churches which minister in areas where significant numbers of asylum seekers and refugees have been housed, have asked themselves how they could show Christian love in practical ways to such individuals and families. As a result, there are significant church-based projects which offer support to asylum seekers and refugees. An example is the Dreamcoat Project in a northern city. This project was the vision of a member of the congregation in a community where, suddenly, large numbers of people were being housed. These people had no real connections to anyone else, and were isolated socially, emotionally and physically. They often did not have enough English language to know how to get by in this country, such as how to apply for a school place or access health care. The project began by offering free English classes, in association with a local college. At the same time, there would be a 'drop-in' held at the church – members of the church would volunteer and cook a hot meal for the beneficiaries.

Very soon, the beneficiaries themselves wanted to cook and contribute. People were welcome regardless of faith and, in time, there were a number of nationalities meeting together – from Zimbabwe, Syria, Iran, Eritrea, Iraq, Afghanistan, Nigeria to name but a few. Significant bridges were being built. Funding was applied for to employ a project manager and project worker. They were able to signpost people to local facilities and help with form-filling, along with able volunteers. Children's activities, football, a clothes store, a computer, health care, all became part of the project, and over the years many other activities were added. Today, beneficiaries are helped to find lawyers, and church people will go with them to court – a sign of Christian solidarity. One user, Neshat, commented, 'Without Dreamcoat I would be lost. I look forward to it all week; my kids too. I am all alone in my flat all week, with no one to talk to. Here I get help. I like to cook too. It makes me feel useful.' As the beneficiaries become more confident, they grow in leadership skills by becoming volunteers themselves and leading activities.

A number, particularly Iranians, having experienced Christian love in action, have actively begun coming to worship at the church on Sundays. As one beneficiary said, 'The church is my family.' The minister commented on how he was touched to see a working-class pensioner buy Christmas presents for refugees in the congregation. At a weekly prayer meeting, members of the church can pray for the needs of those they know of who are going through trauma. About twenty-five Iranians have been baptised, attended Alpha courses, Bible studies, and have been confirmed. They are increasingly a full part of the church community, feeling welcome and valued as individuals made in the image of God.

In the next chapter, we focus on another of the deacons, Philip, who was given a pioneer spirit to go out into new territories to proclaim Jesus to the Samaritans, excluded from ritual worship, and the Ethiopian eunuch, also an outcast.

Action

- Reflect on how you understand prophecy today – whether it is hearing God's utterances to the church and to individuals as encouragement, or speaking out prophetically against injustice.
- Think about the Old Testament prophets, e.g. read through Micah chapters 1 to 3 and research the issues Micah was called to denounce. What do you think Micah would say in our society today?
- Think about when we should speak out against injustice and oppression, in the name of Christ.

- Find out more about the plight of asylum seekers today.
- Can you support a church-based asylum seeker/refugee project? Are there ways to support asylum seekers in your local community?

Endnotes

1. www.archives.gov/files/press/exhibits/dream-speech (accessed 2.12.14).
2. www.archives.gov/files/press/exhibits/dream-speech (accessed 2.12.14).
3. www.archives.gov/files/press/exhibits/dream-speech (accessed 2.12.14).
4. Ben Witherington III, *The Acts of the Apostles, a Socio-Rhetorical Commentary* (Grand Rapids, MI: William B. Eerdmans, 1998), p. 257.
5. Tannehill, *The Narrative Unity of Luke–Acts: A Literary Interpretation* (Minneapolis, MN: Fortress Press, 1990), p. 293.
6. Anthony Harvey, *Asylum in Britain: A Question of Conscience* (Chichester: George Bell Institute, 2009), p. 5.
7. Refugee Council, *The facts about asylum*, http://www.refugeecouncil.org.uk/policy_research/the_truth_about_asylum/facts_about_asylum_-_page_1 (accessed 17.1.18).
8. Nick Spencer, *Asylum and Immigration: A Christian Perspective on a Polarised Debate* (Milton Keynes: Paternoster, 2004), p. 87.
9. Spencer, *Asylum and Immigration*, p. 87.
10. Spencer, *Asylum and Immigration*, p. 100.
11. Harvey, *Asylum in Britain*, p. 60.
12. Harvey, *Asylum in Britain*, p. 73.

8
The Excluded Included

We must restore hope to young people, help the old, be open to
the future, and spread love. Be poor among the poor. We need to
include the excluded and preach peace.

Pope Francis[1]

There are many groups of people and individuals who feel excluded by
society on the basis of their race, their background, their social class
or their status. This was an issue throughout New Testament times.
In Acts 8, we see how an excluded, despised group, the Samaritans,
came to hear the gospel and respond. The chapter begins with great
persecution following the stoning of Stephen. In fact, as happens on
multiple occasions in God's mission, this tragic event became a force
for good. The Christian disciples, the followers of Jesus, young in their
faith, escaped and became scattered across Judea and Samaria (Acts
8:1). This became the impetus to begin mission to the Samaritans.

This marked a change in mission; there is a 'twist' as the emphasis
on key figures changes.[2] The apostles remained in Jerusalem wanting
to keep power. The spotlight fell on Philip, who took up the mantle as
preacher.

Throughout this chapter, we will travel with Philip as he proclaims
Jesus to the Samaritans, then take a brief interlude with Simon the
magician, and finally see the conversion of the Ethiopian eunuch.

The excluded – the Samaritans
The Samaritans were very much an excluded group. Pure Jews,
including the apostles, brought up under strict Judaism would become
defiled through mixing with Samaritans, let alone sharing faith and
worship. Ben Witherington III describes the perception of Samaritans
by most Galilean and Judean Jews (in rather a un-PC way) as 'at best

half-breeds and at worst foreigners', looked down upon and excluded by virtue of their social and ethnic standing: 'They are viewed as ethnically strange and religiously rather heterodox but not simply as pagans or Gentiles.'[3] In 2 Kings 17:24–34 we are told something of the history of the Samaritans: they were immigrants from Iraq who had been forcibly removed to live in the Jewish area called Samaria by the king of Assyria:

> The king of Assyria brought people from Babylon, Kuthah, Avva, Hamath and Sepharvaim and settled them in the towns of Samaria to replace the Israelites. They took over Samaria and lived in its towns. When they first lived there, they did not worship the LORD; so he sent lions among them and they killed some of the people. It was reported to the king of Assyria: 'The people you deported and resettled in the towns of Samaria do not know what the god of that country requires. He has sent lions among them, which are killing them off, because the people do not know what he requires.'
>
> 2 Kings 17:24–26

This was a deliberate political act, aimed at intermarriage so that 'pure' Judaism would be defiled. In addition, the Samaritans brought with them pagan practices. Such history would live long in the consciousness of the Jewish people, and explains the deep-rooted cultural prejudice in their attitudes.

In Luke 9:51–55, we see the antipathy and condescension of the disciples to the Samaritans:

> As the time approached for him to be taken up to heaven, Jesus resolutely set out for Jerusalem. And he sent messengers on ahead, who went into a Samaritan village to get things ready for him; but the people there did not welcome him, because he was heading for Jerusalem. When the disciples James and John saw this, they asked, 'Lord, do you want us to call fire down from heaven to destroy them?' But Jesus turned and rebuked them.

We see here something of Luke's stance – that Samaritans are equally worthy of coming to faith in Christ; that the gospel is open to everyone – all peoples, classes, genders and races.

Luke portrays the Samaritans as 'foreigners', who were therefore generally excluded from formal worship. In Luke 17:11–19 Jesus demonstrated that he saw the Samaritans as worthy of healing and life-changing experiences:

> Now on his way to Jerusalem, Jesus travelled along the border between Samaria and Galilee. As he was going into a village, ten men who had leprosy met him. They stood at a distance and called out in a loud voice, 'Jesus, Master, have pity on us!' When he saw them, he said, 'Go, show yourselves to the priests.' And as they went, they were cleansed. One of them, when he saw he was healed, came back, praising God in a loud voice. He threw himself at Jesus' feet and thanked him – and he was a Samaritan. Jesus asked, 'Were not all ten cleansed? Where are the other nine? Has no one returned to give praise to God except this foreigner?' Then he said to him, 'Rise and go; your faith has made you well.'

In this account, it was the Samaritan, the outsider, who showed the most gratitude to Jesus for his life-transforming experience – he threw himself at Jesus' feet with joyful respect. It was the 'foreigner' who was most commended.

Philip was not affected by human prejudice; his emphasis was on following the prompting of the Spirit:

> Philip went down to a city in Samaria and proclaimed the Messiah there. When the crowds heard Philip and saw the signs he performed, they all paid close attention to what he said. For with shrieks, impure spirits came out of many, and many who were paralysed or lame were healed. So there was great joy in that city.

> Acts 8:5–8

Poverty and condescension

Throughout history there have always been groups who are excluded or looked down upon. I passionately want to see the church of Jesus flourish in the inner cities and outer estates. These are the places of the 'left behinds', the excluded, the powerless. These are communities vilified by the media and on TV. Recently, an inner-city street was portrayed on TV in the programme *Benefits Street*. Local residents felt hard-working people had been misrepresented and class differences perpetuated. The state of the welfare system was also criticised in some of the media for creating a something-for-nothing benefits culture.

Our communities need to be transformed through the love of Christ – away from the negative energy that seeks meaning through gangs, through short-lived relationships, through violence, through frustration, through drugs and alcohol abuse. Yet, the inner cities have great vibrancy – there is a sense of community and identity. Community fun days in neighbourhoods I have worked in have been very well attended – different cultures meet together and share food, fun and laughter. Community cohesion happens naturally. This is not to say that inner cities and outer estates are without tension and prejudice: outer estates in my city often breed extremist parties, overt racism and, in certain areas, Islamic fundamentalism. Yet, my view from multi-ethnic, multi-faith communities is that a great deal has been done in terms of building true cross-cultural friendships. People live much closer together, in tower blocks, or back-to-back houses right on the street. Yes, tensions erupt sometimes, but many significant friendships are formed. In my current context, before I was appointed, the suicide of an asylum seeker who had been forcibly moved to a detention centre resulted in the church holding a moving prayer vigil around the streets of terraced houses where the deceased had lived. The act of worship and remembrance was well attended by the local community, his neighbours – a sign of solidarity and sacrificial love. Because the community knew him, he was not viewed as an 'asylum seeker', a statistic, but as a human being who had lived and moved in their midst.

Victorian churches – then and now

In every city you visit, you will see huge Victorian church buildings. Although much has been documented in recent times about declining church congregations, history records that the established churches never wholeheartedly reached the working classes. The *Faith in the City* report comments on the churchgoing census of 1851, at a time when the Church of England was the prevalent church:

> The Church of England's most enduring 'problem of the city' has been its relationship with the urban working class. Though the cities in general appeared as problem areas for the established Church, it was clearly in working-class districts that the problems were most acute. [4]

The report reminds us that the Church of England never has deeply penetrated the strongly working-class neighbourhoods: in 1851, a religious census established that Anglican Church attendance differed vastly from borough to borough: from 57 per cent in suburban Hampstead to merely 6 per cent in Shoreditch. Horace Mann, the Anglican author of the official report, mentioned the following possible factors as contributing to 'the alienation of the poor from religious institutions':

(i) the social inequalities within the churches: for instance, the system of hierarchically-arranged rented pews;
(ii) the fact that class division in society ran so deep that even if there were no such symbols of inequality within the churches, working-class people would not wish to worship with members of other classes;
(iii) the apparent lack of interest on the part of the churches in the material well-being of the poor;
(iv) suspicion of the clergy because of their middle-class character and comfortable lifestyle;

(v) the effects of poverty: many working-class people lacked time or space for reflection, and were too preoccupied with more immediate problems to give much thought to religion;

(vi) lack of 'aggressive' missionary activity.[5]

Following the wake-up call in 1851, there began a huge building programme of Victorian churches, across all denominations, in working-class areas. During the nineteenth century, over 4,000 Anglican and 20,000 nonconformist churches were constructed, yet attendance was never as high as anticipated – some churches were never more than half-full – although greater proportionally in nonconformist settings. Today we are left with a legacy of huge Victorian church buildings, cold and hard to heat, in our inner-city communities. Many have closed and have become gurdwaras, Hindu temples, community centres, carpet warehouses or flats, but those that remain open for worship are challenged by how they can reach out into their communities and draw people to Christ.

St Mark's is set in an inner city in the north of England: one of thousands of Victorian churches, visible to all around through its spire and millstone edifice. It is surrounded by 1960s tower blocks, and streets of late-Victorian terraced houses, built cheaply for the rapidly rising working classes. By the 1980s the congregation had diminished to around sixty, mainly elderly members. The building was so cold that in winter worship had to take place in the church hall. A new minister arrived and released the church into spiritual renewal, introducing them to a more informal style of worship, open to the guidance of the Holy Spirit. People encountered the Holy Spirit and there was a new sense of joy and hope.

The minister and the church council had a vision to transform the building for the late twentieth century and beyond, as a locus for mission. As Ann Morisy wryly observes:

Our Victorian forebears judged that it was disrespectful to use churches for anything but for worship, and so they filled them with pews to ensure that nothing inappropriate could take place. Today churches are increasingly shaking off this demarcation. Up and down the country congregations have made a great effort to adapt large Victorian churches for flexible use – worship on Sundays and community use throughout the week.[6]

This is exactly what St Mark's did. The hall was sold, and funds were raised. The Victorian edifice was divided into a worshipping space with wooden floor and stackable chairs (no pews) and a narthex area for meetings and community use. New toilets were put in (previously there had been just one), a modern kitchen, two good-sized meeting rooms in the tower and vestry areas, and a new heating system.

The church began a long period of growth. The renewed church building had become more accessible, and community groups could meet in the narthex. The church began a social project for local youth, and employed youth workers. The room in the tower became a computer suite, funded by the council and other trusts, to provide a training resource for the local community in an area where there was no community education. They provided accredited courses and helped people with applications for employment. It became a very popular facility and gave the church a very high profile in the community, along with the youth work, which also provided community education, e.g. on drugs awareness and sexual health. As one local resident commented, 'It keeps the kids out of mischief. The streets feel quieter now; before they all hung around at the corner and people were frightened to walk past.' The church, like many, through its long history and rootedness in the community, has become a major community resource. Through the love shown to them, local people have become followers of Jesus. Just like the early church, they have been baptised and been filled by the Holy Spirit.

A word of warning though – changing a church building into a community centre can result in the church being seen as failing in its primary spiritual task of making disciples. As Morisy explains: 'If the church's commitment to community development is to move people from the foundational domain towards the explicit domain where the deep message of hope through Jesus can be communicated, it has to adopt a purposeful strategy.[7] By this she means that there needs to be a spiritual presence prevalent through the community work. She suggests 'community chaplains', either lay or ordained, who encourage people to 'do business with God', integrate church life with weekday activities, see the church social outreach as a new way of being church, and build up a sense of social capital across church and users.

The old self

We return to Philip, who was unrestricted by social norms. He had been commissioned as one of the seven to help serve the needs of widows. The twelve had not 'authorised' him to preach, let alone to the Samaritans. But Philip could not limit what God wanted to accomplish; his ministry could not be compartmentalised. His ministry of serving led to healings as he took every opportunity to preach the gospel. Philip's ministry brought great joy.

Peter and John were sent by the apostles to Samaria to check out what Philip was up to – but they too were moved by the Holy Spirit and we observe that their innate prejudice towards the Samaritans was challenged – they wanted the new converts to receive the Holy Spirit, so they laid hands on them and many did receive the Spirit (8:17). There then followed a bizarre incident with Simon the sorcerer, who described himself as 'great'. In reality he was someone seeking power and affirmation (and indeed money) through his magic/sorcery. Simon, who had a large following, was convicted by the Holy Spirit during Philip's preaching and joined the many people who gave their lives to Christ and were baptised. Like many people who become Christians, things from the past can still have a strong hold on them – Simon still clearly wanted power, and affirmation from the public, so he offered to pay Peter 'so that everyone on whom I lay hands may receive the Holy Spirit' (vv. 18–19). No doubt he could make money out of this. The early church's view was that money and possessions were a distraction from building the kingdom of God, and 'greed; the attempt to hoard money; the acquisitive, self-centred instinct; and especially the attempt to buy or control the power or blessing of God are sharply condemned.'[8]

Peter had no time for Simon's sinfulness and bitterness – in effect, he said, 'May you go to hell. If your motives are not right with God, you cannot be part of God's leadership team.' Simon was convicted of his wrongful thought patterns and repented: 'Pray to the Lord for me so that nothing you have said may happen to me' (v. 24).

In all contexts, but notably in the inner cities there are many 'Simons' – people who come to Christ, yet the past has too much hold on them. Many church leaders bemoan how much time they spend with people like Simon, helping them to grow in their faith and integrate into the life of the church.

Dayna had started coming to church in her late twenties, following a series of violent relationships. Somehow, she had become addicted to such activities. It surfaced later that she was reminded of her own abusive father, who had disappeared when she was eleven. Each time she became attracted to someone similar, and the pattern was perpetuated. She had one child and began thinking she wanted her child to have a secure upbringing, so one day she turned up at church. She had attended church as a child but had not been for many years. The first time she visited this church – which although small was vibrant, with children, young adults, the elderly, different nationalities and lively worship – she experienced something of the Holy Spirit. She felt shy and guilt-ridden, but something greater than her frail human experience kept her buoyant, and gave her a sense of peace she had not experienced before. She sought counsel and prayer with the pastor, to whom she was able to unburden. The pastor helped her identify patterns in her life and pray through these. All was going well for her on her spiritual journey, until one day an ex-lover turned up at her door. She couldn't say no, and felt trapped again. The pastor and a church elder prayed in her flat, for her protection and for God's guidance on her life. Nevertheless, after a few weeks she stopped coming to church, and before long she had moved away without trace.

For the church community and the pastor this was devastating, but they kept praying. I have heard about countless Daynas: life in the inner city can be tough; mental illness and unhealthy patterns abound. But God is able to do 'immeasurably more than all we ask or imagine' (Ephesians 3:20). Keeping hope alive can be difficult and inner-city/estate ministry can feel demoralising at times, but every small sign of the kingdom is a sign of hope.

To the ends of the earth

Philip was next led to speak to an Ethiopian eunuch, once again breaking social norms. The conversion of the Ethiopian eunuch (Acts 8:26–40) authenticates the 'Great Commission', to spread the gospel of Christ to 'the ends of the earth' (Acts 1:8). His account brings in a new culture: Ethiopia. Herodotus describes Ethiopians as black,[9] but here we are presented not just with someone black, but also a castrated Gentile. Tannehill stresses that Luke is interested in outsiders, e.g. Cornelius, who we will come to, and that he emphasises a gospel for everyone, regardless of religion, race, gender, class or sexuality. We still have a lot to learn from Luke in the church today.

There is a significant sequence of events in this account. Firstly, Philip was prompted by an angel to 'Go south to the road – the desert road – that goes down from Jerusalem to Gaza'. Philip was open to God's guidance, and became God's agent in pushing boundaries, as new groups of people and different races came to an understanding of the gospel of Jesus Christ. Spiritually, he was open to God leading him to wherever God called him to go – on this occasion to the desert road. This may well have been surprising to Philip, but God has a history of calling people to unlikely places to be his agent of mission.

When I left theological college, of twenty new curates, only three went to inner-city contexts, and only one of these to the north of England. In the north of England, it is often difficult to find ministers to fill posts, whereas in the south, there are usually multiple applicants for any vacancy. It is easy to make excuses – reasons cited include the work of the spouse or the education of children. In 1984, Bishop David

Sheppard coined the phrase 'comfortable Britain'. Maybe it is human nature to seek the comfortable option, suburbia, and the leafy market towns. But why do so few people feel called to urban ministry or the outer estates? These are real mission fields, sometimes complex and uncomfortable, but often with a vitality and vibrancy that 'comfortable Britain' cannot offer.

David Sheppard's Dimbleby Lecture in 1984 was ground-breaking. I was still at university and very open to God's preferential option for the poor. To me this lecture was mind-blowing, and highly influential on my call to ministry. Sheppard recounts the lecture, entitled 'The Other Britain' in his autobiography, *Steps Along Hope Street*:

> I spoke of 'Comfortable Britain' to which the majority of us belong, and said there were two Britains today, damagingly divided . . . I said there was a series of doors clanging shut that added up to a poverty that imprisons the spirit – unemployment, neglected housing, lack of good opportunities at school, poor services in health care, transport and leisure facilities. Together these locked doors made very large numbers of people feel powerless and unable to make any real choices about their destiny. The poverty of 'the other Britain' was a priority concern for all of us, and especially for Christians. This priority concern for the poor was not an expression of offbeat radical theology. It sprang out of mainstream Christianity.[10]

Sheppard wrote at a time of great social change, which affected the north of England particularly badly, with the sudden demise of many heavy industries and coal mining. Many communities have still not recovered from this time, and the rich–poor divide is greater than ever.

In a seaside town with much youth unemployment and resulting crime and drug abuse, a number of churches came together with a vision to support young people aged fourteen to twenty-five, particularly with a view to helping them find pathways into work. A shop on the high street was rented, providing an open door where young people could wander in.

At the drop-in there is the opportunity to learn to write CVs, use the internet, and learn to seek work. The drop-in provides free use of the internet, printing, emergency food, support and advice. Many of the users are people who have been in trouble with the law or who are at risk, those excluded from school and the homeless. The Christian ethos is apparent. Support provided is both practical and emotional – often the people coming have complex situations and underlying emotional/behavioural issues, so one-to-one sessions are available, encouraging a change in attitude and behaviour.

The Ethiopian eunuch

As Acts 8 progresses, we are presented with this new character, the Ethiopian eunuch. Luke emphasises the fact that here was a black African, as it 'suits his purposes of showing the gospel reaching different ethnic groups and all sorts of people'.[11] The Ethiopian was probably a Gentile, and because he was a eunuch, would have been automatically excluded from worship. Nevertheless, at the moment he met Philip, he was showing an interest in the Jewish faith, reading from the prophet Isaiah, and was on his way to Jerusalem to 'worship'. We are told that the Ethiopian was an 'important official in charge of all the treasury of the Kandake (which means "queen of the Ethiopians")'. He was a high-powered civil servant, but was inopportunely compelled to be castrated in order to work for the queen. The world was a very harsh place, although we get no evidence of him complaining.

The Spirit prompted Philip to enter into conversation with the man, so he responded immediately and ran up to the chariot. He seized his opportunity to share the love of Jesus without prejudice. He invited the Ethiopian to have a living relationship with Jesus, his sins forgiven by the crucified Christ. The Ethiopian responded at once and asked to be baptised – he had just been reading about the suffering servant, so Philip would have been able to tell him this prophecy had been fulfilled in Jesus. Immediately after the baptism, the Holy Spirit whisked Philip away, but the Ethiopian 'went on his way rejoicing', transformed by his encounter with God, Jesus and the Holy Spirit, and no doubt ready to share his new-found faith with others.

How do we welcome those on the fringes who come seeking faith? One day, three Rastafarians turned up in our church. They had lots of questions, and wanted answers, but carried a lot of preconceived ideas about who Jesus was from their study of Rastafarianism. We invited them to the Alpha course and they came, engaged, asked many questions, and distracted the discussions. But they kept coming. In the Holy Spirit session, one commented, 'That was powerful!' as they experienced the power of the Spirit. They finished the course, but after a while we lost touch with them.

Our Christian response was to welcome them, accept them as they were, as people seeking the living Christ. We were at times tempted to judge them, as they so often were drawn back to Jesus' ethnicity – whether they thought Jesus was black – and kept returning to certain scriptures which intrigued them. This was compounded by the fact that one of the group members had been brought up as a Jehovah's Witness. Philip accepted the Ethiopian eunuch just as he was, and responded to his questions as they came. This is what we did, trusting the Holy Spirit for what to say, and getting it wrong sometimes. But we persevered. We do not know what seeds have been sown, that is God's work, but the idea of not prejudging people is a biblical mandate.

Having witnessed the powerful conversion of the Ethiopian eunuch, the scene is set for the most dramatic of conversions: Saul, the persecutor of the Christians. It is to Saul that we turn in Chapter 9.

Action

- Look again at the three encounters in Acts 8, bearing in mind the marginalised.
- What can we learn about spreading the love of Jesus from Philip?
- Reflect on: 'And what does the LORD require of you? To act justly and to love mercy and to walk humbly with your God' (Micah 6:8).
- Imagine what it means to leave your comfort zone.
- Think about how your church building (if you have one) can be used more creatively for wider mission.

Endnotes

1. Pope Francis on a visit to Palestine, 22 May 2014.
2. R.C. Tannehill, *The Narrative Unity of Luke–Acts: A Literary Interpretation* (Minneapolis, MN: Fortress Press, 1990), p. 102.
3. Ben Witherington III, *The Acts of the Apostles, a Socio-Rhetorical Commentary* (Grand Rapids, MI: William B. Eerdmans, 1998), p. 280.
4. The Archbishop of Canterbury's Commission on Urban Priority Areas, *Faith in the City: A Call for Action by Church and Nation* (London: Church House, 1985), p. 30.
5. *Faith in the City,* p. 30.
6. Ann Morisy, *Journeying Out* (London: Continuum, 2004), p. 183.
7. Morisy, *Journeying,* p. 187.
8. Witherington III, *The Acts of the Apostles,* p. 286.
9. See Tannehill, *Narrative Unity,* p. 109.
10. David Sheppard, *Steps Along Hope Street: My Life in Cricket, the Church and the Inner City* (London: Hodder & Stoughton, 2002), p. 234.
11. Witherington III, *The Acts of the Apostles,* p. 295.

9
Grace for All

We think sometimes that poverty is only being hungry, naked and homeless. The poverty of being unwanted, unloved and uncared for is the greatest poverty. We must start in our own homes to remedy this kind of poverty.

Mother Teresa[1]

Conversion is an act of changing direction. In Christian terms, it is the moment when the living Jesus Christ encounters humanity, maybe at their lowest point – unwanted, unloved and uncared for, as Mother Teresa elucidates. He alone metamorphoses despair to hope and joy. In 1838, John Wesley had reached a point of despair, lacking faith to even preach. He confessed his decision to cease preaching to a Moravian friend, Böhler, who advised Wesley: 'Preach faith till you have it. And then because you have it, you will preach faith.' Wesley was astonished to see a prisoner come to a living faith through his teaching. One day he opened his Bible and came across 2 Peter 1:4: 'Through these he has given us his very great and precious promises, so that through them you may participate in the divine nature, having escaped the corruption in the world caused by evil desires.' He recorded what happened later that day in his journal:

In the evening I went very unwillingly to a society in Aldersgate Street, where one was reading Luther's preface to the Epistle to the Romans. About a quarter before nine, while he was describing the change which God works in the heart through faith in Christ, I felt my heart strangely warmed. I felt I did trust in Christ, Christ alone, for salvation; and an assurance was given me that He had taken away my sins, even mine, and saved me from the law of sin and death.[2]

Saul's very dramatic conversion will set the scene for the mission to the Gentiles. We learn that Saul was born in Tarsus in Cilicia, part of the Greek-speaking diaspora, but the son of a Pharisee and Palestinian Jew, and is a Roman citizen. He was educated in Jerusalem at the feet of Gamaliel, where he learned to be 'faultless' (Philippians 3:6) in the law and exceeded all his contemporaries in diligent study of the law (Galatians 1:14). Quite a mixed upbringing, and we discern in it the roots of his Pharisaic zeal.

Saul moved effortlessly between two cultures: Greek and Hebrew. This crossing of cultures, which in many ways marked Paul's ministry, gave him a strong empathy with different groups. Paul had been part of the group who persecuted Stephen, in his zeal for the law. In his own trial, he said of his own background:

> I am a Jew, born in Tarsus of Cilicia, but brought up in this city. I studied under Gamaliel and was thoroughly trained in the law of our ancestors. I was just as zealous for God as any of you are today. I persecuted the followers of this Way to their death, arresting both men and women and throwing them into prison, as the high priest and all the Council can themselves testify. I even obtained letters from them to their associates in Damascus, and went there to bring these people as prisoners to Jerusalem to be punished.
>
> Acts 22:3–5

Saul was a passionate person; he did not do anything by halves. When he first appeared in Acts, he was zealously persecuting the Christians. He was driven by belief that what he had been taught, the primacy of the Torah with its 613 laws must not be endangered at any cost. When his fundamental beliefs were threatened, the only course of action available to Paul was the attempted wholesale destruction of the perpetrators: 'But Saul began to destroy the church. Going from house to house, he dragged off both men and women and put them in prison' (Acts 8:3). This passion, seemingly innate in Saul, soon became translated into a zeal to bring people to Christ-centred faith, plant churches and see these flourish. As C.K. Barrett explains, 'This was a radical change of religious direction, and it was accompanied by as radical a change of action: the active persecutor became an even more active preacher and evangelist.'[3]

Saul was on his way to Damascus, where he was planning to wipe out the spread of Christianity, through violence. The persecution in Jerusalem had driven many converts out of Judea, but even in Damascus they were not out of reach of the Sanhedrin. Paul, in his zeal to destroy Christianity, had demanded that the high priest should extradite any Christian fugitives to Jerusalem, where they would be imprisoned and then tried.

Suddenly this fervent, determined persecutor had a life-changing experience: 'As he neared Damascus on his journey, suddenly a light from heaven flashed around him. He fell to the ground and heard a voice say to him, "Saul, Saul why do you persecute me?"' (Acts 9:3–4). Saul met Jesus dramatically and suddenly. 'No single event, apart from the Christ event itself, has proved as determinant for the course of history as the conversion and commissioning of Paul.'[4] The risen Christ met with Saul in such a powerful, compulsive way that Saul had no choice but to change direction and follow him. He was rendered blind and had to be led into Damascus by his travelling companions, where he remained blind for three days, neither eating nor drinking.

Damascus was an important city and commercial centre, located on the main trading route between Egypt and Mesopotamia. Its population included a significant number of Jews. In Damascus, through a vision the Lord prompted a Christian disciple, Ananias, to go and meet Saul. Saul himself had been given a vision that Ananias would come and lay hands on him, to restore his sight (Acts 9:10–12). Ananias was of course afraid, as he had heard reports of Saul, the terrible persecutor, who had come to destroy the Christians with the backing of the chief priests. But God reassured Ananias: 'Go! This man is my chosen instrument to proclaim my name to the Gentiles and their kings and to the people of Israel. I will show him how much he must suffer for my name' (Acts 9:15–16).

Saul's mission and calling was becoming clear: God had a plan and purpose for him. Ananias trusted God and did exactly as he asked him. Calling Saul 'brother', he laid his hands on him, and immediately, 'something like scales fell from Saul's eyes, and he could see again' (v.18). Now Saul could see again both physically and spiritually. He had encountered Jesus in the most dramatic of conversion experiences, and turned from the rigid Pharisaic, legalistic faith to the freedom of knowing Christ and possessing the gift of the Holy Spirit to guide him.

What is significant for us is that Saul, or Paul as he later became known, was given a definite mission: to spread the gospel of Jesus to the Gentile world and make the message of Jesus clear to everyone: Jew, Gentile, slave, free, male and female (Galatians 3:28). Thus the mission to the Gentiles was born.

What are we to make of Paul's miraculous conversion experience?

Paul was 'converted' to a view or way of looking at things which he had fought against. As a result, he re-evaluated his life and calling. The drama of his conversion certainly impacted his lifestyle and mission and he used the element of drama in his testimony to emphasise how he had met Christ whilst a sinner. He was called to take Christianity into the world through his missionary journeys, and establish churches wherever he went (Acts 13–14). There is evidence to suggest that he was aiming to create united Jewish and Gentile churches (e.g. Acts 11:19–26). In Galatia, when he wrote his epistle it seems there was a split between Jewish and Gentile Christians (Gal. 3:26–29). In chapters 1 to 3, he was addressing the Jewish Christians about their relationship to the law – he did not abandon his Jewish roots, his aim was to bring all people to Christ. He did not reject his Jewish culture, but his aim was to see the law fulfilled in Christ through Jews accepting Christ: 'To the Jews I became like a Jew, to win the Jews. To those under the law I became like one under the law (though I myself am not under the law), so as to win those under the law' (1 Corinthians 9:20). In reality, his desire to convert the Jews was often unfulfilled, as it was generally the pagans who accepted Christ and not the Jews.

Paul's aims were wider than preaching to the Gentiles or bringing Jews to faith in Christ. Paul saw himself as 'set apart' as an apostle (Acts 13:2), and Paul and Barnabas were 'sent' out as missionaries (Acts 13:4). The descriptions of the missionary journeys give much evidence of Paul's skill as an orator and his determination to preach the message of Christ resurrected to Jews and Gentiles.

Paul's principal aim, apart from being evangelistic, was to see strongly established churches. His letters were written primarily to encourage and strengthen the churches, and at times to reprimand them; he dealt with each church separately, and within their own context, culture and circumstances. Colossians 1:28–29 sums up this aim: 'He is the one we proclaim, admonishing and teaching everyone with all wisdom, so that we may present everyone fully mature in Christ. To this end I strenuously contend with all the energy Christ so powerfully works in me.'

In his life and ministry, Paul suffered many hardships such as earthquakes, imprisonments, hostilities and beatings. Paul's attitude to these was linked to his eschatological view, so that he could experience God's power and demonstrate God's power through the cross and resurrection (1 Corinthians 2:1–5). Luke was closely involved in Paul's work, and as a result gives him much attention in Acts. Luke believed fervently in Paul's mission; he himself accompanied Paul on his missionary journeys. In Acts 16:10 he uses the word 'we' as he describes accompanying Paul to Troas and to Philippi. In Acts 21, he went with Paul to Jerusalem. Paul then became a prisoner for more than two years, and as soon as Paul was about to be sent to Rome, Luke was with him again (Acts 27:1) and he accompanied him to Rome. Paul himself states that Luke was with him during his imprisonment in Rome, telling Timothy, in 2 Timothy 4:11, 'Only Luke is with me'. Luke was a co-worker, faithful and a great support and encouragement, especially during Paul's time under house arrest.

Paul's conversion was life-changing, and a defining moment in the spread of Christianity. The most unlikely convert became the most important missionary, commissioned by God to spread the message of Christ crucified and resurrected.

Conversion – from what to what?

As an evangelical Christian, with my own testimony of conversion, I believe strongly that an encounter with Jesus, crucified and resurrected, can change the direction of our lives. Like Paul, conversion is *metanoia*: an act of encountering Christ, experiencing his forgiveness, and changing direction. In urban areas, people's lives are often very complex, but it has been a privilege seeing people come to Christ, seeking his forgiveness and new life. As with the example of Paul, God can use powerful testimonies of lives turned around to bring others into his kingdom. We will look at some such stories of people who have inspired me with their remarkable journeys of faith.

Jack's story

Jack came to God through asking for help in difficult and stressful situations. Jack works as an electrician and lives in an inner-city community. He tells his story here:

In the past, I had read some verses from the Bible and watched the *God TV* channel. Growing in my faith, I said the prayer asking for forgiveness and for God to come into my heart.

A couple of years ago, when my mum died, I remember asking myself what happens to us when we die. Where will my mum go? At the same time as dealing with the loss of my mum, I was taking care of my dad who was in a home and not able to walk. The pressure got to me and it affected my marriage. As all this was going on, my marriage was breaking down. It was three major events all at the same time to deal with and, eventually, I became low and depressed.

I moved, after separating from my wife, and I wanted a church to go to. While out on a run one Sunday morning, I noticed Emmanuel Church and decided to go to a service one Sunday. I wanted to go to church to find comfort inside myself, learn more about Jesus and worship God. Also, I wanted to meet new people; being depressed, I got very lonely. Going to church was a commitment I knew I had to make if I wanted to be close to God. After attending church for a short while, I went on the Alpha course, which was really good: it has helped me understand, and answered the questions I had about Jesus. I know that by attending church my faith can remain strong and grow. I feel that with the Holy Spirit in me I have got better at breaking my bad habits and sins, which I believe can only be overcome by the power of the Holy Spirit. The anger, bitterness, sadness, loneliness and hurt I felt through loss have all been eased by the Holy Spirit. The knowledge that one day I will go to heaven to be with God gives me a satisfied inner peace. It feels great. The most important and best decision I have ever made in my life was to become a Christian.

Jack's testimony is of an encounter with Jesus that changed him. Jack has become more involved in church life, and is beginning to volunteer. More importantly, his friends and colleagues have started to see a change in him and he has opportunities to share his faith. Sometimes Jack finds the Christian life difficult but, overall, he is on a life-changing journey, which has changed his life for good.

Ola's story

Ola, who is of Nigerian parentage, had been brought up in a big city. This is her story:

My parents separated when I was young, and although they used to go to church, we somehow stopped going. I think my mum was stressed and felt as if people were staring at her. Even though it was a Nigerian church, she felt she was a second-class person because she was on her own. At that time I didn't have a faith to speak of, although I would say I believed in God.

In adulthood I met Ade and we got married and soon we had our first baby. I got a good job in accounts; it was all going well.

Then, I became pregnant again, but my baby died just after she was born. I was at rock bottom, really depressed. We had a funeral in our local church; it was a bit of a blur. I just remember this tiny white coffin. It was terrible. But I remember hearing words of Jesus in the service. The next Sunday I turned up at the church service. I sobbed all the way through and rushed out before the end. I didn't know what to say to people, though they were nice. I started praying. The next week I went again, and found it hard not to cry. In the notices, the curate spoke about an Alpha course the church was about to run. I chatted to the curate after the service and asked if I could attend. She said it was starting that week, at her house. So I went. The first week was a bit hard, but I wanted to learn more. We had a meal, and you could ask questions. I didn't say much. Through the week, and the next week, I started to think about what I had heard. The third week was like a thunderbolt. I felt something inside me at the end – I couldn't explain it. The curate gave us this prayer, asking Jesus to forgive us and give us new life. I said it and felt real peace. I didn't tell the curate straight away, but when I did, she was over the moon! I can really say that my life was changed. I felt a real peace, and started smiling again. I know that can only be God.

A few years later, Ola telephoned the curate, who had now moved to be a minister in another area, and said that she was the churchwarden (a key leader in the church). Ola's faith journey had begun with tragedy, but she had surrendered to God's grace. Her transformation is an ongoing process, and she has become stronger as a Christian, now serving in a position of leadership.

Al's story

Al had a traumatic childhood: he was abused by his father, became violent and often got into trouble. By the age of thirteen he had been expelled from school and, after another bust-up with his dad, ended up running away. He got into gangs, sleeping on people's floors, and began glue-sniffing. Before long, he was smoking cannabis. To fund his habit, he stole and was eventually arrested. He ended up in a young offenders' centre. This was a very harsh environment and, on reflection, Al said this had made him more violent on his release, not less. He did, however, go to some church services and heard some messages that spoke to him. But Al was soon back in trouble again. By the time he was eighteen he was on heroin and was dealing, and he saw his life wasting away before him. Yet, he continued in his old ways, and ended up being involved in a violent clash, which resulted in him being charged with grievous bodily harm and ending up in prison.

One day while he was in his cell, he saw light shining in through the bars, and he heard a voice in his head saying, 'You are my son.' He thought he was hallucinating, but he felt an incredible sense of warmth and peace – something he had never felt before. He didn't do anything about this, but did attend the church services held in the prison more often, even though it meant being mocked. He had been given a Bible and started reading the gospels.

On his release, Al went to find a local church, but found it was closed. He saw the phone number of the minister on the notice board and rang it – the minister couldn't see him there and then, but invited him to come to church on Sunday. But Al couldn't wait. He wandered through the neighbourhood and eventually he found a friendly pastor who helped Al find a living faith. Al's life had been miraculously changed; like Paul, he had seen an overwhelming light, and Jesus had come to him in a vision. Al said this was the first time ever that he had understood what family was. Like Paul, Al changed direction, under the guidance of the Holy Spirit, and now he works as a drugs counsellor and has a number of speaking engagements sharing his story, often to disaffected youth.

As a church, we sometimes lose sight of our primary calling to 'go and make disciples of all nations, baptising them in the name of the Father and of the Son and of the Holy Spirit, and teaching them to obey everything I have commanded you' (Matthew 28:19–20). There are certainly areas and groups of people that are harder to reach, due to their complex lives and, equally, a fear of ministering in what may be perceived as 'tough' areas. Yet God is the God of transformation, the God of all he has made. Saul was an unlikely convert – someone who the Christians were extremely fearful of – yet he became the recipient of divine grace. Jesus met with him miraculously and changed the direction of his life forever. He was richly used by God. It is unlikely that without God's direct intervention the Christians, such as Ananias, would have dared speak to Saul about Jesus, yet Jesus himself met with Saul and used Ananias to explain divine truths.

Each of us is called to be Jesus' agent of grace, to be willing to venture towards the people he draws us to, in order to help them find life-transforming love, acceptance and security. There are many examples of individuals like Jack, Ola and Al, who have encountered the living Christ and whose lives have changed direction. We are called to be available for Jesus, praying for opportunities to see despair change to hope. To see unlikely people set on fire for God and serving him, however God calls them, is great encouragement, and Jack, Ola and Al have all been used by God. Conversion is not an end in itself, but a beginning – the whole spiritual process of nurture, growth and service are the Christian's life-calling. Paul's life-calling was made very clear, despite opposition. It is not always straightforward to follow Christ, as Paul himself found.

In the next chapter, the scene is set for the mission to the Gentiles, largely through Paul. We first return to Peter, who himself had a 'conversion' experience in which his innate prejudices were confronted by the Holy Spirit.

Action

- Think about your own journey of faith. What were the times when you have been most energised?
- Reflect on what you understand by the word 'conversion'.
- It is life-enriching to serve God in difficult situations. Recall times when God has taken you into difficult situations. How did this affect your faith?

- Spend some time with Paul. He went on to serve God with inspired enthusiasm, in areas where many fear to tread. Read Acts 21 – what you observe about God's mission through Paul?

Endnotes

1. motivationalreads.com/think-sometimes-poverty-hungry-naked-homeless (accessed 25.1.18).
2. John Wesley, *Journal of John Wesley*, Christian Classics Ethereal Library, www.ccel.org/ccel/wesley/journal.vi.ii.xvi.html, (accessed 17.1.18).
3. C.K. Barrett, *A Critical Commentary on Acts: Vol. 1* (Edinburgh: T & T Clark, 1994), p. 442.
4. F.F. Bruce, *Paul, Apostle of the Free Spirit* (Exeter: Paternoster Press, 1977), p.75.

10
No Favouritism

God's dream is that you and I and all of us will realize that we are
family, that we are made for togetherness, for goodness, and for
compassion.

Desmond Tutu[1]

Human nature and sinfulness has led to division and condescension
– often on the basis of race, class or gender – rather than for God's
ideal of 'togetherness, for goodness, and for compassion'. If each of
us is honest, we all hold some idea of prejudice and favouritism. In a
satirical TV comedy, an upper middle-class woman began her political
campaign with the slogan: 'No tattoos in Waitrose!' demonstrating a
bias against people she viewed negatively.

Where do we show favouritism? Who are the people we discriminate
against? Welcome these people as you would Christ, as James reminds
us in his epistle:

> My brothers and sisters, believers in our glorious Lord Jesus Christ
> must not show favouritism. Suppose a man comes into your meeting
> wearing a gold ring and fine clothes, and a poor man in filthy old
> clothes also comes in. If you show special attention to the man
> wearing fine clothes and say, 'Here's a good seat for you,' but say to
> the poor man, 'You stand there' or 'Sit on the floor by my feet,' have
> you not discriminated among yourselves and become judges with
> evil thoughts?
>
> James 2:1–4

In the 1840s, William Booth preached in The Bottoms, the most
depraved slums of Nottingham. Having engaged people with Jesus, he
persuaded a number of very poor men, women and children to come

to the Broad Street Methodist Church. They reluctantly came and he directed them to seats at the front. Their clothes were ragged, smelly and dirty. Booth believed that in spite of their appearance they would be welcomed, but in reality not a single church member even spoke to them. In fact, men and women covered their faces with handkerchiefs and turned away. On the way out the minister, Reverend Dunn asked Booth if he might speak to him. Reverend Dunn admonished Booth, saying that the poor were to enter by a side door and sit on the benches allotted to them, out of sight.[2]

Most churches would not admit prejudice or favouritism, but prejudice is a complicated issue to define and even more difficult to deal with. The story of the good news spreading beyond Jewish boundaries towards the Gentiles teaches us, through the life of Peter, that there is no favouritism in God's kingdom, and that God must break down prejudice if effective mission 'to the ends of the earth' is going to take place (Acts 1:8).

Peter's vision

By Acts 10, the message of Jesus transforming lives had spread to Jews, Samaritans and those outside traditional Judaism (Acts 2:39; 3:25). Luke significantly locates the conversion of Saul just before the moment where Peter was called to be the ambassador of the Gentile mission. Saul (Paul) was to be the great, passionate missionary to the Gentiles. We now return to Peter, who was challenged by the Holy Spirit about his religious and cultural prejudices. Once Peter's conceptual breakthrough had taken place, he was in a position to inculcate the Gentile mission into the Jerusalem elders.

First, though, Peter had to be confronted about his prejudices. As David Seccombe observes:

Peter was no Pharisee, but even an ordinary Jew was scandalised by the thought of the contamination attendant on eating defiled food. Social intercourse with Gentiles carried the same stigma. If there was any thought at this stage in the apostles' minds of a mission to the uncircumcised it certainly did not include joining them in table fellowship prior to their baptism, circumcision and cleansing.[3]

Peter went up to the roof of Simon the tanner's house, where he was staying, to pray. At the same time, Cornelius, the Gentile centurion, sent messengers to find Peter. This is a very carefully constructed drama. Whilst praying, Peter became hungry – something I am sure we can all identify with. Whilst praying, distractions may come back and forth: we need another coffee, there's another email to check, the phone rings. It is reassuring to know that Peter, the great church leader and missioner, also became distracted whilst praying. Peter then 'fell into a trance', which we may interpret as being full of the Holy Spirit, and received a vision concerning food. The spiritual importance of the vision is emphasised by Luke through his use of apocalyptic language: Peter saw heaven open and something like a large tablecloth being let down by its four corners. This is symbolic of the cloth being lowered down to all four corners of the earth. This was a catalytic event in the history of the world – Jesus for everyone will be proclaimed aloud.

The tablecloth was filled with creatures – all kinds of four-footed animals, reptiles and birds. Peter was well versed in Leviticus 11, where 'clean' and 'unclean' animals are distinguished. Peter certainly would have felt contaminated if he had made any contact with unclean animals, so when he was told to 'Kill and eat', his natural response would have been to say no, which he did. Even though he was addressing God in his 'no', he clearly thought that he was being tested. But God responded telling him that that nothing he has made is unclean. Peter is shown the vision three times – Seccombe compares this to Peter denying Jesus three times.[4] Peter was being transformed in his attitudes to other races: the unclean food that Peter was then able to touch represented the people that Peter was to approach with Jesus' gospel – no one was unclean in God's sight.

In a dramatic illustration, Peter is called to live out his new learning immediately. Peter is divinely prompted to enter into Cornelius' house. Cornelius is a centurion from Caesarea. Peter would have previously seen it as 'unlawful', that is outside Jewish law, to associate closely with other races (Acts 10:28). But Peter's prejudice had been challenged, and the Holy Spirit was giving him a gentle prompt, more akin to a kick up the backside, to get right into Cornelius' house: not to merely pop in for a moment, but to stay for a few days. Later, he was criticised by his fellow Jews: 'You went into the house of uncircumcised men and ate with them' (Acts 11:3). But something powerful had happened: 'More is achieved here than the conversion of a Gentile. Close association and table fellowship are established, implying brotherhood in a radically new people of God.'[5]

Peter was challenged not to discriminate against Gentiles – the Greek word *diakrino* means discriminate. Strict Jews prided themselves on making distinctions between right and wrong. 'I now realise how true it is that God does not show favouritism but accepts from every nation the one who fears him and does what is right' (Acts 10:34–35).

Then, in a spiritual encounter mirroring Pentecost, as Peter explained the gospel of Jesus Christ, the Holy Spirit came in great power upon all who were gathered there:

> While Peter was still speaking these words, the Holy Spirit came on all who had heard the message. The circumcised believers who had come with Peter were astonished that the gift of the Holy Spirit had been poured out even on Gentiles. For they heard them speaking in tongues and praising God.
>
> Acts 10:44–46

So we have yet another example of the link between the Holy Spirit and social transformation. Peter's faith was no longer privatised or exclusively for 'the circumcised', those 'in' and favoured. The Holy Spirit is not merely a private experience, an experience to build the person up in faith. This is part of the work of the Holy Spirit, but the Holy Spirit plays a part in the transformation of society and challenges unjust structures and ways of thinking – in this case, racism.

The nature of racism

In Peter's transformational encounters, there is much for us to reflect on today, particularly with regard to racism and prejudice. Racism operates at three levels: overt, covert and institutional.

In my recent visit to South Africa, I was brought to reflect anew on the fallacy of overt racism, through exploring the effects of apartheid on the church today, twenty or so years after the 'new' South Africa was born. Deplorable as it seems, apartheid was constructed on a particular fusion of nationalistic political theories and an idiosyncratic theological position. Certain Old Testament passages were used to justify the Afrikaner position as a 'chosen nation, set apart to do God's work'. The key passages are: the Tower of Babel in Genesis 11 – that God has ordered division of the races; Deuteronomy 32:8 – the concept that God had given each nation its inheritance and the nations were divided, and God 'fixed the bounds . . . according to the number of the sons of God' (RSV). In other words, this proliferates the idea that the Afrikaners are the chosen and favoured race, with whites being Christian and blacks the heathen. This demonstrates the profound and destructive dangers of basing a theology on a limited number of texts and justifying these as a means to an end. Tutu points out that such selective and narrow reading of the Bible fails to see the Bible as an entity.[6] For example, using Babel as a key text, Afrikaners repudiated reading the Bible in the light of Pentecost – the Holy Spirit bringing all people back together.

The Afrikaners, profoundly shaken by the Boer War, were led to a battle for survival. The way they did this was through creating 'apartness' or apartheid. In 1948, apartheid was officially born. It lasted until 1994, forty-six years, and, despite all the rhetoric that healing and reconciliation has taken place since 1994, there continues to be after-effects on the moral, spiritual, economic, political and cultural spheres of South African society.

In 1950, the Group Area Act came into being. This operated on three levels: facilities and amenities such as public transport, cinemas, beaches, homes and business activity. Father Michael Lapsley, who arrived in Durban as a priest from New Zealand in the 1970s, was stunned at public signs: 'There were two entrances, one saying "Whites only" and the other, "Non-whites".'[7]

On a larger scale, the populations were to live in separate and distinct areas. Blacks, Indians and Coloureds each resided in their own 'townships' or areas where they alone could live. This was a deliberate political system – apartheid structures were based upon racially divided 'zones', with buffer strips between them to discourage mixing. Blacks were forced to live in substandard townships, with poor quality housing and often no sanitation or running water, on the very outer rims of the city. Huge inequalities were imposed by apartheid's laws; there was, and remains at many levels, a massive chasm between those who are extremely poor and the massively rich.

Many church denominations in apartheid times became more and more vociferous about the injustice and inhumanity of apartheid. Michael Lapsley, arriving as a young chaplain to Durban University, was urged into action as a result of his Christian faith: 'For me, that compass has always been the Christian gospel that calls upon us to act on behalf of human dignity and justice, no matter what the consequences.'[8] His outspoken critique of the apartheid government resulted in him being banned from South Africa, at first to Lesotho, where he joined the ANC, and then to Zimbabwe. 'Consequently, the liberation struggle in South Africa was from the very beginning for me a matter of faith. Apartheid was a system that killed the souls of both white and black people in contravention of God's will.'[9]

In 1990, in Zimbabwe, three months after Nelson Mandela was released from prison, Lapsley was sent a letter bomb by the South African security forces. It was hidden inside two religious magazines. In the blast, he lost both hands, the sight in one eye and was seriously burnt. He now works for reconciliation and forgiveness, as Director of the Forgiveness Foundation, based in Cape Town. His book is aptly titled *Redeeming the Past: My Journey from Freedom Fighter to Healer*. Despite losing his hands and being partially sighted, he is remarkably resilient. My wife and I had the privilege of meeting him. He is testimony to the brutalities of the apartheid government, which routinely used violence. He writes of himself:

> When I walk the streets of South Africa, my appearance confronts people with the truth of who we are as a people and what we've done to each other. So, yes, I am a sign of triumph over adversity, but I am also, with my humanness and my limitedness, a sign that compassion and gentleness are stronger than evil, hatred and death. This is possible for all God's people in the fullness of their humanity, and not just for a sainted few.[10]

Racism in the UK

Racism in the UK is more subtle. This is a subject close to my heart, as I was born in Britain to parents who emigrated from India, as I have already mentioned. I was the first generation of British Asian, and I had to work out my identity, which was not always easy. I have had a very British upbringing, but also have had strong Indian influences. I am proud to be Indian, and love India profusely. When Lord Tebbit introduced the 'cricket test', saying that those living in Britain were only truly British when they supported England at cricket, I instantly began supporting India. I love India, but I have spent almost all my life in the UK, and it is here that I feel called to usher in God's kingdom.

Race is a complex subject. It defines who we are. Britain has been multicultural and multi-ethnic for centuries, with conquests by Normans and Danes, which have all brought different cultures into the UK – in fact, there is very little that is pure British. Since the 1950s there has been much greater immigration into the UK, and this has created a rich, diverse and overall accepting society, particularly in the cities. Yet racism still abounds. Recently 'immigration' has been a hot topic, as more and more intolerance has crept in of migrant workers, refugees and asylum seekers. Economic migrants seek a more comfortable life.

We must not forget the legacy of colonialism – the major movement of people into the UK in the 1950s and 1960s was from the former colonies. Anthony Harvey refers to an indictment by the former Archbishop of Canterbury, Rowan Williams of the colonial legacy:

> To a great extent (as Archbishop Rowan Williams remarked not long ago) the refugee problem is a problem of our own making. Not just the slave trade, but the systematic exploitation of the resources of Asian and African countries in the colonial era made the developed countries permanent debtors to the world. Refugees from poor countries may be seen as people coming to reclaim the inheritance of which they were robbed during centuries of western rule and domination.[11]

By the end of the nineteenth century, 'Great Britain' had colonised a quarter of the world. It therefore seems to me to be unsurprising that people from the former colonies and elsewhere want to come to the UK. Our Christian response must be repentance and reconciliation in face of the enormous problems in the world that colonial legacy has left behind. This includes much of the world's conflict through policies of 'divide and rule'. The ongoing tensions between India and Pakistan are just an example; this ill-thought-out British policy of 'partition', placing Hindus and Muslims into separate homelands, even though for centuries they had somehow managed to live together, resulted in the unnecessary deaths of half a million people.

In the immediate post-war years, there were successive waves of people coming to work in the UK from the former colonies. My parents, who arrived in the 1950s, came with an inbred understanding that Great Britain was the 'mother country' – the enormous, imperious statue of Queen Victoria in Kolkata is a vivid symbol of this. Here the 'Empress of all India' looks down at her subjects, and they look up to her as the great benefactor. When people arrived from the former colonies, they were expecting a warm welcome at the heart of the mother country. Sadly, almost the opposite was true, and the church was not exempt, we are now ashamed to say.

Covert racism generally takes place when individuals do not believe they are racist but hold stereotypical views, such as with 'refugee' which has at its root 'seeking refuge'. It has become sabotaged by some sections of the media who use the term to refer to people who have come to grab more for themselves, perceived as 'bogus' and 'fake' and a threat to moral order. In my community, currently such people are often blamed for the decline of the community and for any petty crime that takes place, whereas in reality there is a whole spectrum of people involved in crime.

Such views are very common in the tabloid press and easily become part of common parlance. More subtle assumptions that can seep into the church are that all Africans are late to church or that Flo's from X country, so we can't trust her on the rota. On the other hand, people may stereotype Afro-Caribbean boys by saying, 'They're good at sport, we'll let them in our football team,' which is condescending. The result is a mental blockage and an incapacity to see someone's true merits. Unconscious racism, like our body odour, can cling to us without us knowing it. In the church, racism will not be admitted, but covert racism is played out all the time. It is often hard to prove, and those who complain may be told they have a 'chip on the shoulder'. For ministry, we may let black people make tea, but we don't let them read 'because of their accent'.

As regards selection for ministry, the process can be particularly difficult, and although many steps have been taken to address this, there is still far to go. The selection system for ministry in many churches is still based upon a middle-class, 'educated' way of thinking. When I have sponsored ministry candidates without formal qualifications, I have encouraged them to go on courses and develop a theological understanding first. Candidates may be told they are reserved, but they are from cultures where it is not polite to be forthright. As with many areas, mentoring and support is the key to enabling black, Asian and minority ethnic members to find their full potential.

The term 'Institutional Racism' was coined following the murder of black teenager Stephen Lawrence in 1993. Allegations of racism and corruption within the Metropolitan Police were investigated by Sir William Macpherson. In fact, he made a damning report defining institutional racism as:

> The collective failure of an organisation to provide an appropriate and professional service to people because of their colour, culture, or ethnic origin. It can be seen or detected in processes, attitudes and behaviour which amount to discrimination through unwitting prejudice, ignorance, thoughtlessness and racist stereotyping which disadvantage minority ethnic people.[12]

It made seventy recommendations, many aimed specifically at improving police attitudes to racism, and stressed the need for a hasty increase in the numbers of black and Asian police officers.

As Christians, whatever church we belong to and whatever denomination, we have to ask whether our church is racist in any form: overtly, covertly or institutionally. This debate is currently taking place within the Church of England, my own denomination. Fairly recent data showed there were four clergy from black or minority ethnic backgrounds in what are termed 'senior' roles (bishops, deans, archdeacons), which represented just over 1 per cent of the total number of senior appointments, compared to 3.5 per cent of active Church of England congregations.[13]

The House of Bishops' theological statement 'Affirming our Common Humanity' affirmed a commitment to ethnic diversity in the senior leadership of the church. The report asserted that 'Christians should celebrate the diversity found in the human family' and acknowledged 'the universal bond that human beings are all made in the image of God, equal in dignity, sharing a common humanity in which God shows no partiality or favouritism'. It also recognised that 'the Church of England is committed to share the gospel and the life of the kingdom across cultures and ethnicities' and that 'our witness, our worship, the nurturing of our congregations, our care for the world and our service of our parish communities are all better in themselves and more fully reflect God's glory for being led and undertaken by men and women of diverse backgrounds'.[14] The church is positively taking steps to introduce more black clergy into senior roles, but it is a slow, arduous process. Nevertheless, there has been much to celebrate and there are now a third more BAME (Black and Asian Minority Ethnic) clergy in senior roles.

Today, in Britain, racism is highly complex and is not just black against white. This is a serious issue the church needs to engage with. UKIP (UK Independence Party) have recruited Indians, and have promulgated them on TV adverts to attempt to show that it is a party open to all, and not a racist party. It wants to distinguish itself from far right parties such as the BNP (British National Party) to make it more acceptable. Currently they are succeeding in this aim. Yet their underlying ethos is that Brexit Britain operates best as an island cut off from Europe, in charge of its borders and in control of who is invited in. It is my opinion that this was how the Empire operated, yet if you conquer half the world, you can hardly be surprised when half the world wants to come to Britain. Our past actions do have consequences to them.

Living in an area where there had been many different waves of immigration, I observed how the newest community arriving became the scapegoats. Racism is very subtle, and is not just white on black or vice versa. The comedian David Baddiel, who is Jewish, commented on how he received a racist tweet, calling him a 'Jewish *****'. When David Baddiel questioned the tweeter, he received the reply: 'I can't be racist, I'm a Pakistani.'[15] In Southall, I had to question Indians and Caribbeans, who had themselves been the victims of racism, but now felt established, about their negative stereotyping of Somalis, the new community to arrive there.

A guilty past

When the first people came from the former colonies, their experience of the mother country was far from what they had imagined. Most scandalous was the attitude of the church in many spheres. Eunice was a member of a congregation in London. She had been a lifelong Anglican; her father had been a proud churchwarden in Barbados, a respected member of his community and church. When Eunice arrived in London in the 1960s, she naturally went to her local Anglican church, dressed in her Sunday best and hat, as she had always done. She was surprised that when she sat down in church, people stared at her and no one sat near her. At the end of the service the vicar said to her, 'If you come back again, then sit at the back,' and pointed to the back corner aisle pew. Fortunately, Eunice did go back, and was not going to be intimidated. Soon she moved to an area where a larger number of black people lived, and here the vicar had a deliberate policy to welcome all. Today that church is thriving and growing, thanks to the numbers of members from black and minority ethnic backgrounds. Eunice became a stalwart of the church and, like her father before her, a churchwarden.

Others were not as resilient as Eunice, and many joined black Pentecostal churches where they felt safe. This is a tragic loss to many churches today. In his study of *West Indian Migrants and the London Churches* in the 1960s, Clifford Hill found that about 70 per cent of West Indians had belonged to traditional churches but only 4 per cent continued to attend such churches.[16] As a result of this racism, both overt and covert, the Pentecostal churches grew rapidly. In some cases, people found the welcome cold in sparsely populated churches with no sense of community.

Today there are significant numbers of multi-ethnic churches. In the next chapter we will look at how churches can truly reflect diversity and how we may interact with other cultures and faiths.

Action
- Read through the story of Peter's vision and how the Holy Spirit challenged his innate prejudices (Acts 10).
- How may we create real sense of community that genuinely crosses barriers?

- Spend some time thinking about your own areas of unconscious bias and prejudice.
- Find out more about what it is like for someone to experience racism – overt, covert or institutional. What do you think is the New Testament response?
- How can Christians be more culturally aware, like Saul himself, whose own prejudice was broken down by the Holy Spirit? He would travel far and wide to preach Jesus Christ: 'but we preach Christ crucified: a stumbling-block to Jews and foolishness to Gentiles' (1 Corinthians 1:23).

Endnotes

1. http://www.godhasadream.com/media/Desmond_Tutu_Q_and_A.pdf (accessed 25.1.18).
2. See T. Yaxley, *William & Catherine* (Grand Rapids, MI: Bethany House, 2003).
3. David Seccombe in I. Howard Marshall and David Peterson, *Witness to the Gospel: The Theology of Acts* (Grand Rapids, MI: William B. Eerdmans, 1998), p. 360.
4. Seccombe in Marshall and Peterson, *Witness*, p. 360.
5. Seccombe in Marshall and Peterson, *Witness*, p. 361.
6. D. Tutu, 'Christianity and Apartheid' in J.W. de Gruchy and C. Villa-Vicencio (eds), *Apartheid is a Heresy* (Cape Town: David Philip, 1983), pp. 39-47.
7. Fr Michael Lapsley and Stephen Karakashian, *Redeeming the Past: My Journey from Freedom Fighter to Healer* (Maryknoll, NY: Orbis, 2012), ch. 5, location 931, Kindle.
8. Lapsley and Karakashian, *Redeeming the Past*, location 669.
9. Lapsley and Karakashian, *Redeeming the Past*, location 702.
10. Lapsley and Karakashian, *Redeeming the Past*, location 516.
11. Anthony Harvey, *Asylum in Britain: A Question of Conscience* (Chichester: George Bell Institute, 2009), p. 60.
12. Home Office, *The Stephen Lawrence Inquiry: Report of an Inquiry by Sir William Macpherson of Cluny*, Cm 4262-I, February 1999, para 6.34. Advised by Tom Cook, the Right Reverend Dr John Sentamu, Dr Richard Stone.
13. See www.churchofengland.org/2016ministrystatistics.pdf (accessed 25.1.18).
14. 'Affirming Our Common Humanity: A theological statement by the House of Bishops' (General Synod, 2011).
15. www.theguardian.com/commentisfree/2014/dec/02/antisemitism (accessed 3.12.14).
16. Clifford Stanley Hill, *West Indian Migrants and the London Churches* (Oxford: OUP, 1963).

11
Without Prejudice

Prejudice

Noun:

Preconceived opinion that is not based on reason or actual experience:

'English **prejudice against** foreigners'

'deep-rooted class prejudices'

Dislike, hostility, or unjust behaviour deriving from preconceived and unfounded opinion:

'accusations of racial prejudice'

Oxford English Dictionary

As we have seen, to hold prejudice is to pre-judge an issue; it is to hold an opinion on that subject that has no real factual basis. It has been formed through the way we have been conditioned or brought up. Peter's vision resulted in him being thoroughly challenged about his own prejudice, following which he found himself at the centre of a storm. It is a bit like being called to a government enquiry for an act of conscience. The believers criticised him both for entering the house of the uncircumcised and for actually eating with them. In Jewish thought, this would have made Peter ritually unclean. Fortunately, Peter had the opportunity to defend his position, and did so without being defensive, and with great joy and spiritual maturity.

For Luke, this is a key moment in the history of Christianity – a turning point for the full force of the Gentile Mission. 'The apostles and the believers throughout Judea heard that the Gentiles also had received the word of God' (Acts 11:1). Later in Acts 11, Barnabas went to fetch Saul from Tarsus and took him to Antioch to help him build the church, teach and make disciples: 'The disciples were called Christians first at Antioch' (v. 26). Much of the rest of Acts covers the story of

Saul/Paul and his missionary journeys, leading people to Christ and planting churches.

Peter encounters prejudice

The Jewish Christians were not happy that Peter had made himself unclean by entering the house of uncircumcised Gentiles and eating with them. At this point, as far as they understood, only those who were circumcised could be true believers. Later on there was a debate about Gentile converts needing to be circumcised before they could be a full part of the church.

There is an interesting parallel with the church today. What conditions do we put on people when they come to church? In the past, certain standards of dress were expected; certain forms of behaviour. In a small estate church, a single struggling mother with noisy young children was stared at then told to take her children out by church members. She left and did not come back. Fortunately, she did find another church where children were welcome. But many do not return to church at all. If the church is closed, like a club, where worship is conducted in a certain way for the benefit of a few, the church will not and cannot grow. It takes a great deal of courage for someone to walk through a church door, especially on an estate, as in my example. If such a person, who may be carrying a great deal of baggage, is not accepted as they are, then they cannot begin their faith journey. Jesus is being kept from them; they are being excluded.

A multi-faith world

Peter re-evaluated what he understood of God's grace and, in Acts 11 was called to explain to the church in Jerusalem what he had been shown by the Holy Spirit. He challenged the Jerusalem church to break down the boundaries of who's in and who's out, what's clean and unclean. The church elders began by being suspicious about Peter spending time and eating with people of other faiths, but 'when they heard this, they had no further objections and praised God' (v. 18). God alone breaks down barriers.

The fact that we in the UK live in a pluralistic society cannot now be questioned. In terms of our relationship to other faiths and cultures, we need to ask ourselves whether we view some cultures with suspicion.

Many parts of our cities and other towns are 'global villages' where people from many different nationalities, faiths and cultures live together. Here is the ethnic breakdown of one northern inner-city area, based upon Neighbourhood Statistics:[1]

Group (all people)	Value
White British	657,082
Largest minority ethnic group(s):	
Pakistani	15,064
Indian	12,303

Religion (all people)	Value
Christian	492,656
Buddhist	1,587
Hindu	4,183
Jewish	8,267
Muslim	21,394
Sikh	7,586
Other	1,530
No religion	120,139
Religion not stated	58,060

In this area, 39 per cent of the population have defined themselves as being from different parts of the world; there are significant numbers of other faiths, about 23 per cent of which are Muslim. There are many areas like this in the UK. As churches, we are required to ask ourselves: how do we respond to other faiths within our communities? Fortunately, the era of mutual suspicion has passed, and in general people embrace the multicultural vision and richness of these communities. However, we cannot underestimate that in much more segregated towns, particularly in the north of England, there are tensions between

Muslims and white British. On a visit to one northern town, I was able to see how successive housing policies have led to distinct areas: Asians from Pakistan, largely in the old terraced housing; white British, for a large part, on ex-local authority estates. Recently, another area has become favoured by people moving from Poland and other European nations. That there are tensions cannot be denied: certain areas become heartlands of extremist parties, whilst young Muslims may be tempted by more fundamentalist ideologies. This leads to a very unhealthy state of affairs, based upon suspicion and confrontation.

On the Isle of Dogs, after a BNP councillor was elected, it was the churches that led the campaign to ensure he was not re-elected in 1994. The churches of all persuasions worked together with other faith groups, such as the Bengali Action Group and the Samuda Women's Centre, as well as trade unions, to campaign against the BNP. The strategy began with a concerted effort to pray and prayer-walk, instigated by a Baptist minister. A practical action was to encourage as many people as possible to vote, particularly those groups who had felt powerless to vote before, like Muslim women. Susie, a local Baptist minister, recounted to me how she was proactive in driving carloads of people to the polling station. Another strategy was a church engaging in practical action through employing a hands-on community worker.[2] Kenneth Leech identifies that the people who had voted BNP felt disempowered, neglected and ignored, having fallen for extremist politics. This campaign was successful and within six months, the BNP lost the seat.[3]

As churches, we have a duty to teach biblical principles and educate people who may fall into the trap of voting for extremist parties. A few years ago, I was part of a 'Hope not Hate' campaign to educate people against the dangers of voting for extremist parties in west Leeds. At this time, I encouraged the congregation to vote, and explained why the BNP's values were against those of the church. This encouraged people in the church that may have been tempted to vote BNP, who perhaps felt left behind and disempowered by mainstream politics, and also encouraged church members to speak to others in their friendship groups and families. The campaign was successful at the time, but racial hatred is an ongoing issue in many communities, sadly exacerbated following the EU referendum. In my own community there were a number of attacks on people from Eastern Europe, verbal and physical, immediately after the referendum. The local church school organised a community event to celebrate diversity, to challenge hostile attitudes.

Navigating a multi-faith society

There has been much suspicion of Islam in recent times, increased by the growth of terrorism by ISIS/IS (so-called Islamic State). Two days after the 11 September 2001 attacks on the twin towers in the USA, two Turks were attacked on the London underground by football supporters who began to throw them down the escalators. This is an overt form of prejudice against a whole grouping of people by virtue of their race or skin colour, and seeks revenge on unknowing victims. This is little different to Kristallnacht in Hitler's Germany in 1938, when riotous German mobs destroyed almost all signs of Jewish presence. A total of 1,350 Jewish synagogues were burnt to the ground or destroyed, ninety-one Jews were killed, 30,000 Jews were thrown into concentration camps, 7,000 Jewish businesses were destroyed and thousands of Jewish homes were ransacked. This was called 'Kristallnacht' meaning 'the night of broken glass' because the streets were covered with broken windows.[4]

The rise of what has become known as 'Islamophobia' is harmful to Muslims and to good community relations in all areas but, poignantly, particularly where large numbers of Muslims reside. Those involved in extreme forms of Islam are a small minority. As Leech points out, 'The majority of Muslims in most British towns have no contact with these movements, and tend to belong to more devotional, revivalist and politically conservative streams of Islam.'[5]

Chris is a pastor in an area with a high Muslim population. He is very committed to building strong relationships with the local Imam and the Muslim community. He would attend Eid celebrations with a few members of his church, and some Muslims came to church social events. Strong friendships were built up in an area where there were many inter-faith tensions. Chris and the Imam became good friends; they would have breakfast together and talk about the area, and how they could work together. Chris is from an evangelical charismatic background and shared his Christian faith when he could. Chris and the Imam became a symbol of unity in a climate of suspicion. They worked with the council and other partners to build community cohesion and dispel prejudice, being key players on the council's strategic board, working with schools and community centres, where they held community fun days, bringing communities together. Chris told me, 'Relationships are key. Nasser the Imam and I are great friends. Over the years, great trust has been built up between us. We eat together and talk about our faith. People see how close we are and it impacts the whole community. It takes time and we have to work at it. We choose to and it's paying off.'

I recently met Tom, a minister in an area that is 75 per cent Muslim, some settled (from Pakistan) and some new communities. The remaining 25 per cent is a mixture of Eastern European and a small white British community, often older and less mobile. This is part of my interview with him:

Tell me about the vision of the church.

The church's vision is to be salt and light in our multicultural environment: worshipping, welcoming, witnessing. The church has clear evangelical roots; the core of the church live in the community and feel called to live incarnationally.

How do you relate to your community, as a church?

We run a successful English Language Project (four days a week) in the church building. This reaches more than thirty ladies, all Muslims. We also hold craft classes. Traditionally, these women have stayed at home but are finding that they need basic English nowadays. The project was set up when the church perceived a need in the community and wanted to bless and serve the community. In a moving gesture of thanks, a number of Muslim ladies cleared the garden. It's as if they were saying, 'This is our local church.' We also go round door to door giving out copies of the *Jesus* film and having chats with people. Our church runs a debt advice centre. About 98 per cent of the pupils in our church school are Muslim. A church member goes in to school to help with reading. I take Christian assemblies. We hold a successful holiday club every year. These are ways to share the love of Jesus Christ.

How have you built relationships with your local mosques?

We built strong relationship with the local madrasa (college for Islamic instruction). A few of us have engaged in 'scriptural reasoning' – a group of five Muslims/four Christians, we look at a text accepted in common (e.g. Old Testament) and discuss what our faiths have to say about it. We also build relations with the Advice Centre; we meet local community leaders and build bridges.

How do you face the challenges of reflecting Jesus in this context?

It's fundamentally about trying to spread Jesus – the key words are 'presence and engagement'. Church is about good news to share.

Building positive working relationships with all faith communities is fundamental to Christians in a context when the world is coming to us. The notion of 'inter-faith dialogue' has become dated, and I agree with Leech that: 'It often suggests a disconnected, middle-class, rather intellectual activity which is cut off from the mass of the people, both inside and outside the faith communities.'[6] I have found that building friendships naturally can dispel a lot of prejudice. Where we lived previously, we had Hindu neighbours on one side, a Sikh family on the other, a Muslim family and a South African family behind (we all shared a drive). The conversations we had were natural, generally not about faith, but sometimes they were, and we could have genuine discussions without compromising what we believed. On many occasions, a Sikh or Hindu would wander into church and would genuinely request prayer, often for healing. I have been touched by the openness and hunger for prayer. In the project my current church runs for refugees and asylum seekers, people of different faiths often ask me to pray for them. Recently, we prayed with a young Iraqi Muslim, in Jesus' name; she was genuinely seeking to encounter God. We are showing Jesus' love in action, as Paul reminds us: 'I am not ashamed of the gospel, because it is the power of God that brings salvation to everyone who believes: first to the Jew, then to the Gentile' (Romans 1:16).

One of the most fruitful ways of working creatively with others is through some joint working or a shared project. I have been involved in community organising and I have found this to be a very positive way of working together with other faiths and community groups on a common objective, to bring some kind of improvement to the local community. Community organisers work with local communities – churches, temples, gurdwaras, mosques, trade unions, and schools – to listen and distil the issues facing people. They will then mount an 'action', such as a picket, and local people are empowered to campaign, trying to build a relationship with those who have the authority to make changes.

Here is an example of a campaign that brought different faith groups together. Following the murder of an eleven-year-old boy in an inner-city community, different faith groups worked together to find a way of creating safe havens. The project was spearheaded by a local priest, and with the help of a community organiser, Father Tim built on his strong contacts with the local mosque and other community groups. Encounters were set up between people of different faiths, nationalities and languages, creating opportunities for friendship where once ignorance and suspicion had a hold. In all, thirty volunteers from diverse backgrounds were recruited to take part in the campaign.

The second stage of the campaign involved the creation of a number of community 'safe havens', where people running away from violence could find refuge. To achieve this, two action days were organised, where local residents went out in pairs to talk to local shopkeepers and businesses about the issues behind the campaign and to ask whether they would consider being a safe haven.

Wherever possible, volunteers went around in multi-faith pairs, with Christians working alongside their neighbours from the mosque. This has enabled relationships to deepen between ordinary members of the community who would not usually interact with each other. Father Tim acknowledged that if the campaign was to achieve its aims, 'It's critical to show that this is a project of the whole community.' The businesses all agreed to display a sign in their window to signal they were part of the local network of safe havens. Their involvement committed the owners and managers to offer sanctuary to anyone that needed it, locking the door and calling the police if there was a threat of violence.

A diverse church

In the New Testament church, diversity was both normal and healthy; individuals were offered roles on the basis of their spiritual gifts, not their skin colour. In Acts 11:19–28 we get a snapshot of the lively church in Antioch. It was here that Paul began his ministry, mentored by Barnabas. Antioch was a cosmopolitan, multicultural city and Christianity spread rapidly. It was the Roman provincial capital of Syria and a vibrant, successful commercial centre. The culture in Antioch included a significant Jewish community, Romans and pagans. It was in Antioch that the Gentile mission began in earnest. 'Some of them . . . men from Cyprus and Cyrene, went to Antioch and began to speak to Greeks also, telling them the good news about the Lord Jesus. The Lord's hand was with them, and a great number of people believed and turned to the Lord' (11:20–21). In Antioch the Gentiles followed Christ, without the expectation of the need to follow Jewish religious practices, e.g. circumcision and food laws. This was not without controversy, as Peter's encounter reminds us, but the

Jerusalem church sent Barnabas as their trusted leader to oversee the church in Antioch. Barnabas, the great encourager, saw the potential of the church in Antioch – he is described as a 'good man, full of the Holy Spirit and faith'; he affirmed that God's grace was quite definitely at work: 'When he arrived and saw what the grace of God had done, he was glad and encouraged them all to remain true to the Lord with all their hearts . . . and a great number of people were brought to the Lord' (11:23–24).

The church in Antioch was truly diverse; this was the first time the believers were called 'Christians', and the growing Christian community included Jews, Syrians and North Africans. The Antioch church truly modelled a multicultural leadership: 'Now in the church at Antioch there were prophets and teachers: Barnabas, Simeon called Niger, Lucius of Cyrene, [and] Manaen (who had been brought up with Herod the tetrarch)' (Acts 13:1). There is Barnabas, from Jerusalem; Simeon 'called Niger' which in Latin means black, from North Africa in all probability; Lucius of Cyrene in North Africa, today known as Libya; Manaen, of Middle Eastern origin, brought up in Herod Antipas' court; and Saul himself, of strict Jewish parentage but living in the Roman province of Tarsus – a truly multicultural team. These leaders were prophets and teachers, and the church can most definitely be described as 'charismatic', open to direction from the Holy Spirit. This group of leaders laid hands on Saul and Barnabas as they set out on the great missionary journeys, spreading the saving love of Jesus. 'While they were worshipping the Lord and fasting, the Holy Spirit said, "Set apart for me Barnabas and Saul for the work to which I have called them." So after they had fasted and prayed, they placed their hands on them and sent them off' (Acts 13:2).

Towards a multicultural church

As Britain has become more multicultural and multi-ethnic, so fortunately has the congregational make-up of many churches. After the woeful lack of welcome for the first influx of Christians from the former colonies, by the 1990s there was a definite sea change, and a new influx of people moving to the UK from African countries, notably Nigeria, Ghana, Zimbabwe, Uganda and Kenya, found themselves more welcome in the traditional denominational churches. Many, however, chose to worship in more Pentecostal mono-cultural black churches, although in London, in particular, there is a significant African presence in the traditional churches. In many cities and towns, multi-ethnic congregations are now much more prevalent. This is both healthy and enriching. The church is becoming more welcoming, but there is still a long journey to travel. A church with at least 10 per cent black or minority ethnic membership is defined as 'multi-ethnic'.[7] Other churches may have 90 per cent BAME membership. As David Haslam explains:

> Superficially many multiracial churches are splendidly happy families. Black people often bring the kind of outgoing warmth and friendship into a congregation that is sometimes lacking in almost white congregations. However it is important to look below the surface to check that all is as it seems . . . Who greets those who arrive for Sunday morning worship? What proportion of the preachers, worship leaders and junior church teachers are black? Are there black images around the church? And perhaps most importantly, who holds the key offices? . . . When one raises these kinds of questions in a multiracial church the responses can often be hurt and anger, from black people as well as white.[8]

It is true that there is a vibrancy in the multicultural churches that I know and have worked in. It is a powerful witness to see different nationalities genuinely embracing each other, sharing fellowship and Holy Communion, affirming that we are all the body of Christ. Once a culture of welcome is established and there ensues a friendly reception of people of different cultures – engaging in conversation, helping all feel part of the fellowship – then it is likely that people will stay and begin to feel part and included. A church member said to me recently: 'I enjoy the church. It's an exciting place to be as God is bringing people in from different countries. I'm learning more about God's world.' This includes an awareness of the traumatic things that are happening in some parts of the world, e.g. people who have fled persecution. At the baptisms of Iranians and Iraqis, I encourage testimony, which is always a very moving means of learning how God has worked amidst persecution. When one member of the congregation faced deportation, people of all cultures rallied around her, signed petitions, wrote to the MP, and went to her court hearing. Later she said, 'Without the church I would never have coped.' The church members saw this woman as one of their fellowship; a valued member of the body of Christ in that locality.

There is a real sense of being a 'reflection of heaven' in being part of a multicultural church. As some cultures may be less reserved in their cultural preferences, diversity enriches the whole life of the church. In most non-Western cultures it is normal to have meals together; this can impact the life of the whole church, as barriers are broken down, and people interact with others in an informal setting. Diverse food from different cultures creates a wonderful cultural experience, and at such meals there will be much laughter and joy. However, it is not always straightforward creating a truly multicultural church, and there needs to be an intentionality about it. In cultures such as those from the Indian subcontinent and the Caribbean, family times and community are essential aspects of how people respond to each other: meals together are seen as normal; hospitality is a given. If you 'pop in' to see a family or church member, more often than not, you will be offered elaborate snacks, even a meal. This is closer to the New Testament model, where sharing in meals and hospitality was central to how the church operated. This is how true community was formed. In the West, lifestyle is much more individual and we live much more isolated lives.

In one church, where there were three main cultural groups – Afro-Caribbean, Indian and white British – at meals together people would stay in their own cultural groups. In some ways this is a natural human reaction, but it does not reflect a sense of being a united body of Christ

– we are 'all one in Christ Jesus' (Galatians 3:28). In this church, there was a community worker who, with the pastor, was passionate about creating a church without cultural barriers. At the meals together, she introduced games and quizzes that encouraged different people to mix, and break out of their comfort zones.

Cliques can and do develop in any church, and cliques developing along ethnic lines may seem natural. However, one cultural group may become dominant, and be seen as the leaders. Another group may then feel they do not fit in, or excluded. In one church, nearly all the elders were from one particular culture, which made those of other cultures feel like church attenders rather than full participants in the life of the church. In this particular church, the minister set out deliberately to challenge this viewpoint and encourage a wider cross-section to stand for election. This took some time, as the dominant group felt threatened and tended to 'vote on' people they knew well, usually from their own family or culture. The minister also taught about how important it is that the church leadership reflects the diversity of the congregation – that this was both biblical and healthy. Gradually the culture of the church changed and the leadership became more diverse. The house groups, always sharing food, became more diverse, and true cross-cultural friendships were created. Three people, all from different countries of origin, went on an inter-church leadership training course and built strong, lasting friendships. They also became much more confident as leaders in the church: one became a preacher, another a group leader, another an elder.

Service in our churches needs to be monitored for diversity. Who is involved in the welcome team? What about the music group? Who leads at the front? What images of people do we show on our PowerPoints? Are these culturally diverse? If the church is multicultural, the church should strive to reflect diversity in all that it does. As a church we need to empower those who feel weak or inadequate. Spending time mentoring people also pays off. A minister of Indian origin told me how he was called to full-time ministry: 'It was because my pastor believed in me. He spent loads of time with me, and helped me see what I could do. He helped me plan sermons, then gave me feedback. I just became more affirmed. Before, I used to look at the person at the front and think, not me!'

In the next chapter, we will see how Peter encountered a different form of prejudice: persecution of Christians and Herod's paranoid mind, which resulted in him being imprisoned again. But divine power is far greater than human evil, and another awe-inspiring miracle takes place.

Action

- Spend some time with Peter in Acts 11 – how did he confront the prejudice of others?
- How did the Holy Spirit bring about radical change?
- Do you agree that we are often flawed in our understanding because we can only see issues through our culturally conditioned eyes?
- How can we engage with other faiths, whilst not compromising our Christian beliefs?
- Think about how the early church shared Jesus with people from different faiths and backgrounds, e.g. Acts 17.
- What practical steps can be taken to truly reflect God's diversity in all areas of church life and leadership?

Endnotes

1. Statistics compiled by the government reflecting indices of deprivation in each community, www.ons.gov.uk/help/local (accessed 4.2.15).
2. Kenneth Leech, *Race* (New York: Church Publishing, 2005), p. 77.
3. BNP is the British National Party, an overtly racist political party, most active 1982 to 2014.
4. See https://jfedsrq.wordpress.com/category/social-justice/page/2 (accessed 27.1.18).
5. Leech, *Race*, p. 137.
6. Leech, *Race*, p. 139.
7. David Haslam, *Race for the Millennium* (London: Church House Publishing, 1996), p. 182.
8. Haslam, *Race for the Millennium*, p. 183.

12
My Chains Fell Off

Amazing Grace, how sweet the sound,
That saved a wretch like me.
I once was lost but now I'm found,
Was blind, but now I see.

John Newton (1725–1807)

The well-loved hymn 'Amazing Grace' was written by the former slave trader, John Newton, who found a living faith and freedom through a life-changing encounter with Jesus Christ. In 1748, as captain of a slave ship, steering the ship through a turbulent storm, he experienced what he was to refer to later as his 'great deliverance'. He recorded in his journal that when it seemed that all was lost and the ship would sink, he exclaimed, 'Lord, have mercy upon us.' Later, in his cabin he reflected that God had spoken to him, and that grace had begun to work in his life. It was a life-changing moment, and in fact led Newton to give his life to Christian service, eventually being ordained.

In this chapter we begin with a great miracle – Peter is once again imprisoned, this time by Herod, but is set free as his chains fall off through the intervention of God. We will then look at how people today can be held in chains, for example through mental illness, and what response we, as Christians, can bring.

Peter's chains fell off - quite literally

In Acts 11, God's Spirit was moving in the city of Antioch, enlarging the scope of Christian mission. We see how that city was being shaken by the presence of these Christians in its midst. In chapter 12, the church in Jerusalem was being persecuted, with violent, threatening attacks. 'It was about this time that King Herod arrested some who belonged to the church, intending to persecute them. He had James, the brother of John, put to death with the sword. When he saw that this met with approval among the Jews, he proceeded to seize Peter also' (Acts 12:1–3). This was the year AD 44. We can date it because of the date of Herod's death, also recorded here. The church had been growing and spreading during the past eleven years, and James must have been an important leader in the church, although his name has not been mentioned previously in the book of Acts. He is the brother of John, and it was these two men who came to Jesus with their mother and asked to be granted positions at the right and the left hand of the throne of glory when Jesus came into his kingdom (see Matthew 20:20–24). When James was beheaded, the church was stunned. So, when Peter was arrested, there was great concern and earnest prayer was made on his behalf. Herod was afraid of something, too, because he took special care to see that Peter was held as securely as humanly possible. He entailed four squads (Acts 12:4), sixteen soldiers in total, to watch this one man.

In this chapter we will consider mental illness, and Herod Agrippa, like his father before him, is a pertinent case study. He suffered considerable paranoia: he was paranoid about how the powerful Jewish leaders would see him and went to extreme measures – the death of James – to court their favour. It is also probable he suffered a degree of schizophrenia, having delusions of his power and grandeur, even believing he was a deity himself. He was erratic in his moods and unpredictable in his behaviour. Only God could deal with this kind of deranged ruler. There are plenty of examples of modern-day rulers displaying mental illness, who had an adverse effect on their country's health. Indian friends of mine, doctors, in fact, were expelled from Uganda by Idi Amin in the 1970s. Idi's paranoia was such that he believed the Indians were too wealthy and too powerful. No doubt Herod was afraid of the spread of Christianity in his land.

Peter found himself imprisoned by Herod. But God intervened and a great miracle took place. Peter's chains literally fell off:

Suddenly an angel of the Lord appeared and a light shone in the cell. He struck Peter on the side and woke him up. 'Quick, get up!' he said, and the chains fell off Peter's wrists.

Then the angel said to him, 'Put on your clothes and sandals.' And Peter did so. 'Wrap your cloak round you and follow me,' the angel told him. Peter followed him out of the prison, but he had no idea that what the angel was doing was really happening; he thought he was seeing a vision. They passed the first and second guards and came to the iron gate leading to the city. It opened for them by itself, and they went through it. When they had walked the length of one street, suddenly the angel left him.

Then Peter came to himself and said, 'Now I know without a doubt that the Lord has sent his angel and rescued me from Herod's clutches and from everything the Jewish people were hoping would happen.'

Acts 12:7–11

Peter may well have expected to be executed, so when the angel came, Peter was taken by surprise. This can only be seen as a supernatural rescue: the angel took no notice of the guards whatsoever, but simply woke Peter up and the chains fell away from Peter's wrists.

Once Peter realised he was free, he went to the house of Mary, where the faithful were gathered together, in prayer. A servant came to the door. She recognised Peter's voice, and in her excitement forgot to open the door and instead ran in to tell the others that Peter was standing there! They thought she was out of her mind (rather reminiscent of the disciples after the resurrection, when Mary and Mary Magdalene brought news to the disciples of their encounter with Jesus). When they eventually opened the door, they saw Peter and were amazed. Calming them down after their frenzied excitement, he described how the Lord had brought him out of prison. This is a powerful testimony of the power of prayer, and the supernatural power of God conquering evil.

We are told that Herod died a sudden death for believing himself to be a god and because he 'did not give praise to God, an angel of the Lord struck him down, and he was eaten by worms and died' (Acts 12:23). He did not acknowledge the one true living God, and consequently was brought to a just end.

Amazing grace

When an individual encounters the power of grace in their life, their lives are changed forever. The chains that hold many today are not physical but emotional. Jim had a difficult childhood. By the age of twelve, he was in trouble for petty crime. Soon it escalated to violent crime. As a violent criminal, he found himself in detention centres. He said that in his violence he used every kind of weapon; he was into all kinds of criminal activity. As a teenager, he became caught up in drugs and drug dealing. He lived for the moment. He fell in love, married and had children, but secretly he carried on drug dealing.

I asked him how he felt at this time. He said his life was quite empty, but he knew nothing else. He did care for his wife and children but was unsure how he should show affection, due to his background and upbringing. His wife suddenly left one day; he later found out she had been having an affair. Jim's life reached rock bottom, and he became depressed.

In what can only be seen as miracle, Jim found himself on a busy beach with his young children, when an itinerant evangelist came up to him and asked if he thought God was real. He replied, 'No!' and became abusive. Quite randomly, Jim shouted out into the sky, 'Watch this. If there is a God show us a sign,' at which point his young son ran up the beach towards him, shouting, 'Dad, look at this stone, it's shaped like a love heart.' 'Oh yes,' he replied, taking the stone from him, and he told him to go play. As he was throwing down the stone, it flipped over and Jim felt goose pimples on his arms as he saw that on the other side of the stone was a cross.

My first reaction was to think I was going to be struck down. I looked up in silence. There was my sign. He had heard me. As I put the stone in my pocket I felt a bit unnerved, but on our way home, I went into a charity shop and asked for a Bible. The man said they didn't sell them, but said that he had one to give away. I put it in my pocket and went back out to the kids. That night, when everybody was in bed I got the Bible out. It opened at Psalm 118:22 and this is what I read: 'The stone the builders rejected has become the cornerstone'. I knew, despite my ignorance, that this really was God talking deep into my heart.

Jim described how he felt a lightness and an inner peace, but could not define it. He began by asking God if he was real and he gave his life to Christ, asking for forgiveness and a new start. He felt forgiveness – it was a supernatural experience. God helped him change direction. His 'chains fell off'.

But Jim was caught up in a spiritual battle. When he first went to church, he found people staring at him. He was accused of stealing money from the church, summoned to the minster's home and asked to leave the church. People with stories like Jim's need the church to show acceptance and welcome. As Jim will say himself, change is difficult. But God did change him. He became a powerful witness, helping others with complex pasts to find Christ.

This is a story of Jesus ministering to all people, with their emotional pain, baggage and insecurities. The church has to be there for people like Jim, not to condemn but accept. It needs to be there pastorally, listening, praying and supporting practically.

Jim married again and became involved in a local church, experiencing the healing power of the Holy Spirit. Sadly, when his second wife left him, his life fell apart and he struggled with God, feeling anger and abandonment. He stopped going to church.

Years later, through his son experiencing a miraculous healing, he found himself going back to church, seeking to renew his relationship with God. The local church supported him. It was not always easy, as

Jim continued to face problems – emotional insecurities, family issues, financial worries and loss of job.

There is a great need for emotional healing in the church today. It is poignant when individuals come to faith, but we need to have resources to provide the right support to help them find true freedom. I accept that this is not an easy or straightforward process. There is a spiritual battle going on in the lives of many people, particularly with those who have not had an easy start in life. If someone has not had the basic human needs, such as William Temple (Archbishop of Canterbury, 1942–44) outlined, their life will have cavities which will need healing. Temple was instrumental in creating the welfare state, an inspiring example of prophetic Christian leadership. He outlined the six Christian objectives he saw as basic human needs:

1. The material – that all are housed in decency and dignity, and offered proper care. The basic needs such as shelter and food/water are met.
2. The spiritual – all children should be entitled to education which allows them to develop fully. Temple emphasises the spiritual dimension – that education should be inspired by faith in God.
3. The physical – all citizens should have enough work to grant them security, shelter and dignity.
4. Self-esteem – citizens should not be seen as a means to an end in the workplace, they should have a voice and be treated with dignity.
5. The physiological – all people should have access to leisure, time to pursue interests, and personal/spiritual renewal.
6. Self-actualisation – all people should have the freedom of speech and worship.[1]

I add that self-actualisation is achieved only when someone can embody the highest potential that they are capable of reaching. This can only come through being set free by Christ.

Those who have not had access to these basics need to be able to unburden their pain, be listened to and prayed for. This takes time and expertise. Often, trained Christian counsellors can provide the best help.

Mutesi had been brought up as Christian in Uganda but now lived in England. She attended a local church, but soon found her years of pain surfaced. She could not sleep and she became depressed, so she took antidepressant medication. At work, she found it difficult to concentrate, and inner anger would surface, often with her young children. Her husband had left her, which had affected her self-esteem, and she felt looked down upon within her community. As a child she had been abused, physically and sexually, and the memories continued to surface and haunt her. One day, in a house group meeting, she suddenly broke down. The couple leading the group felt out of their depth, but prayed with her, and asked her if she would speak to the pastor. She agreed, and she met the pastor and his wife the next day. She did not open up at first, but they continued to meet with her, seeking God's peace and discerning the guiding of the Holy Spirit. Once she did begin to open up, they realised that they should refer her to trained Christian counsellors. Gradually, Mutesi began to find a new peace, freedom and inner healing. She still falls into depression at times and is not yet free from antidepressants, but she feels stronger in her faith, and has been encouraged by the support and love of her church family. Of course, Christians do not try to solve all Mutesi's problems. They support her in her spiritual and emotional needs, but Mutesi still needs to see her GP and has seen a psychiatrist.

In ministering to the marginalised and the poor, it is inevitable that we will encounter many people with very complex issues. This is because often people's lives have been complicated. They haven't had fair chances early on. They may have encountered social problems or mental health issues. They may feel powerless, as they may not have the resources or resilience to deal with the council, the benefits people, and the Job Centre. But God is for them. Jesus alone can change lives. It may be a difficult journey, and some may find it too difficult, they may find they pray and prayer doesn't seem to be answered. But God is there. As Christians, we need to stand with those who hurt, help them to come to a living faith, be filled with the power of the Holy Spirit, find healing – and then to find a purpose, to serve God through being transformed by the Holy Spirit, to grow as disciples, to share and preach Christ crucified. As Peter proclaimed to the household of Cornelius: '[Jesus] commanded us to preach to the people and to testify that he is the one whom God appointed as judge of the living and the dead. All the prophets testify about him that everyone who believes in him receives forgiveness of sins through his name' (Acts 10:42–43). It is draining sometimes. It can be frustrating, even upsetting, when people struggle to grow in their faith, when you spend months with someone helping them find faith, then one thing draws them away. But in the Acts of the Apostles, it was not easy either. Being a Christian is not purported to be easy for anyone – we are highly aware that we are in a spiritual battle.

Church and mental illness

A church based on an estate found there were a number of isolated people living in their community struggling with mental health issues. The minister, Joan, tells her story:

> I was approached by a worker from a secular mental health charity, as they were keen to have a centre on this estate. A number of people had wandered in to church and wanted to speak to me about their depression and stress. A few congregation members had a passion for this work, knowing how isolating mental illness can be. We asked for volunteers and held a course of training sessions, including listening. The final session included prayer and spiritual reflection.
>
> We planned to meet on Monday afternoons in the church hall. As this is a modern 1970s building, the church and hall connect and we wanted people to see the Christian symbols and be able to go in to pray if they wanted. In fact, people used the church library a lot and often asked for Bibles. We ran an appeal to local churches, as we didn't have much money. We advertised the centre in local GP

surgeries and the worker did so by word of mouth. After the first year, the worker moved on, but we asked for funding from a Christian fund, and were successful, so we employed our own worker. We believed it would work because we knew there was a real need for somewhere for folk experiencing stress and depression to meet in a relaxed setting. We do different activities – art and crafts, sewing, creative writing, reading stories and poetry, and playing board games. Spiritually, we are not overt in our evangelism, but I pop in most weeks and often have a chat. Some of the users do come to services at times and we invite them to Christmas and Easter and special events. The church prayer meeting on Thursdays prays for the project.

Action

- Spend some time thinking about the prayer life of early church, following the death of James and Peter's imprisonment. What is the place of honesty in prayer?
- List what you consider the 'prisons' many face in their life today. It may be helpful to look at Christian resources that may help people begin to find freedom in Jesus Christ.
- It is useful to research local resources and services you can signpost people with mental illness to. Discuss how to pray for and support those suffering mental illness safely in your church.
- Reflect on the Christian doctrine of hope. It is hope alone that will sustain us, it is hope that will see the flickering light even in the darkest situations; it is hope that will point us to the resurrection and the gift of the Holy Spirit.

Endnotes

1. See William Temple, *Christianity and Social Order* (London: Penguin, 1942), pp. 96–97.

Conclusion

To conclude, let me highlight the key themes that I have drawn out through this book and leave you with some final questions and challenges to reflect upon and pray about.

The kingdom of God

Throughout Acts, we are given a wonderful, supernatural vision of the kingdom of God. The kingdom is a gift from Christ, bought through his death and resurrection and sealed by the Holy Spirit (Acts 2:36–38). At the heart of the kingdom is the miraculous: signs and wonders, healing and empowering; the Holy Spirit breaks into this world *now*, to demonstrate that God is indeed ruler of the world he created. The kingdom of God is here – *now*. We can choose to enter it, or not, and as we have seen, thousands did. The kingdom of God is for everyone. Throughout Acts it spreads from Jerusalem to Samaria and the ends of the earth. It was, and still is, for everyone. We need to ask: who are excluded from the kingdom today?

In Acts 1 and 2, Jesus sent his Spirit to empower his followers to be his witnesses and heralds of the kingdom (Acts 1:8). The Holy Spirit has effected countless earth-shaking miracles, from the day of Pentecost onwards, to demonstrate the reality of the kingdom. The kingdom brings people into relationship with Jesus Christ, fills them with the Holy Spirit and turns round the direction of their lives. This is repentance – *metanoia* – a total change of direction. There is another vital and much overlooked dimension to the kingdom of God – that all Jesus' followers should be his agents who bring about change and transformation in this world. It is not just about waiting for the second coming – the *parousia* – when God's kingdom will be truly fulfilled. As Christians, we must bring in the kingdom now, through acts of mercy and sacrificial generosity, so that poverty and dehumanisation, which have no part in God's kingdom values, are wiped out.

Challenge: How do you see the kingdom of God? Is it about personal salvation or is it about radically changing society? What difference can you make? Think about ways your church and you yourself could meet needs in your community, where there is deprivation or poverty. Maybe you will be challenged to leave your comfort zone and seek God's guidance about being incarnational in an inner-city or estate context. Jesus calls us to the ends of the earth, to all places and to all peoples.

Generosity

At the end of Acts 11, there is a touching and powerful interlude concerning sacrificial generosity, which in many ways embodies Luke's vision of justice:

> During this time some prophets came down from Jerusalem to Antioch. One of them, named Agabus, stood up and through the Spirit predicted that a severe famine would spread over the entire Roman world. (This happened during the reign of Claudius.) The disciples, as each one was able, decided to provide help for the brothers and sisters living in Judea. This they did, sending their gift to the elders by Barnabas and Saul.
>
> Acts 11:27–30

Luke's vision of the kingdom does not allow for suffering caused by hunger or lack of material resources. The prophecy here is not a feel-good state of encouragement, but an act of discerning God's concern for the suffering. For Luke, poverty is almost always caused by human greed and the creation of unjust structures in society; these are constantly challenged. Generosity is at the heart of Acts – sharing all material possessions so that no one was left in want (Acts 2:42–47; 4:32–35), caring for the widows and those in need. The admonishment for misusing resources is highlighted (Ananias and Sapphira).

Challenge: How generous are we? Are we sacrificial in our giving? Do we really think about the poor in the world and in our own society? People in many churches have been challenged to act, to give to food banks, to set up night shelters, and in many other ways. We can prayerfully reflect more about poverty in areas of our land, and about the challenges of ministry in the inner-city areas and estates of the country. It is increasingly difficult for churches in these communities to run and deliver projects for the benefit of their communities. If you happen to be in a wealthy church or a suburban area, I challenge you to leave your comfort zone. Perhaps you could partner with a church in a more deprived context and support them – there is much you can learn as well as giving. I have been touched recently by how a very wealthy church has opened their hearts as well as their pockets to learn from, and support, a project for asylum seekers and refugees. Acts encourages us to look outwards – wouldn't it be wonderful if wealthier churches could fund youth work or other projects in the inner city, not wanting anything back, but just giving sacrificially?

Dependence on God

The early church was caught up in a spiritual battle. We are too. At several stages, as the kingdom of God advanced, the apostles found themselves under attack: arrested, harangued, tried, imprisoned, murdered. This was nearly always at the hands of the established religious or political authorities of the day. Luke portrays the Sanhedrin as stubborn, paranoid, hard-hearted and autocratic (Acts 4:1–7). The power they wielded was a false one, and their refusal to accept guilt for the death of Jesus, and even more astonishing, to accept the witness of the resurrection and the miracles of the Holy Spirit, left them looking like pathetic, power-crazed megalomaniacs. Through the power of prayer, through communion with Jesus, by means of sacrificial sharing, and through mutual support and fellowship, the apostles showed no fear in the face of adversity. So strong was their trust in the power of the Holy Spirit and a God who answers prayer that they remained focused on the task that Jesus has called them to. Each time a great miracle took place, the believers gave praise to God (e.g. Acts 4:23–25) and, despite opposition, the number of believers increased by thousands.

The place of prayer and praise is paramount in Acts. Through their fellowship, sharing meals, Holy Communion, reading Scripture and praising God, the believers were encouraged and strengthened for the next stage of God's work. After the death of Stephen, and great persecution of Christians, the scope of mission was enlarged. It was the Holy Spirit who gave Philip and the other apostles the boldness to proclaim Christ to the Samaritans and Ethiopian (Acts 8).

Challenge: How do we seek God's vision for our churches? As we depend on God for his vision and seek his guidance for our mission, we are challenged that everything has to be rooted in deep prayer. I am drawn to the way the apostles worked together in partnership, sharing and praying together, mutually, co-operatively and communally. In our postmodern culture, leaders especially, but also many Christians, work alone. How can we build structures that will better support our work? This is particularly important for those working in 'tough', urban contexts: maybe multi-faith, maybe highly post-Christian, probably beset with crime, violence, racial tension, drugs, mental health and dysfunctional relationships. In these contexts, church leaders and members need much encouragement and good support mechanisms. I ministered in a context where the leaders and members of churches met regularly, prayed for each other, shared vulnerabilities and prophetically prayer-walked round each community. The result was that we were encouraged to persevere, and we all saw growth in our churches, both spiritual and numerical. Is there someone you can support and encourage, working in an urban or estate environment?

God's kingdom is open to everyone

Acts begins with Jesus promising power to his followers, power to spread his gospel to the ends of the earth: 'You will receive power when the Holy Spirit comes on you; and you will be my witnesses in Jerusalem, and in all Judea and Samaria, and to the ends of the earth'

(Acts 1:8). Through the course of Acts 1–12, we read of the apostles and disciples beginning to preach to the Jews of many ethnicities, then the Samaritans, who were very much scorned, and finally the Gentiles (all people), and the process of mission 'to the ends of the earth' has begun.

Gradually prejudice is confronted and broken down so that a truly diverse church of all God's people can be built. Significant moments are Pentecost itself, when suddenly the separatism of Babel is inverted, as the sign of all nations coming together, the foundations of a new global church. In chapter 8, the Samaritans are included – until then very much an excluded group. They respond and come to faith in Christ. Finally, we spend a sizeable amount of time with Peter's dream and its outworking (Acts 10–11), when Peter's own prejudice and unconscious bias is confronted directly by God. This marks the onset of the mission to the Gentiles following the conversion of Saul, who will be its main proponent.

I have outlined many tragic cases from human history where racism has marred God's purposes, and this certainly is far from over. In a world of considerable tension, of civil wars, of a rise in religious terrorism, worldwide migration is at an all-time high.

Challenge: Do we see those fleeing war and religious fundamentalism as human beings created in the image of God? Or are they just statistics, someone else's problem? Are there ways we can respond to asylum seekers arriving into our communities? Some Christians have offered empty houses to refugees; I know some who have deliberately bought a house to rent out cheaply to refugees, an intentional ethical act. Other churches have collected clothing for those arriving or those in camps – one church recently collected fourteen tonnes of clothing to be shipped to Iraq, a huge response from the local community as well as churches.

We all have unconscious bias:

Unconscious bias affects every area of our lives. Unconsciously, we tend to like people who look like us, think like us and come from backgrounds similar to ours. Everyone likes to think he or she is open-minded and objective, but research has shown that the beliefs and values gained from family, culture and a lifetime of experiences heavily influence how we view and evaluate both others and ourselves.[1]

Are there people we view differently because of their ethnicity, social class or race? The early church became a wonderful classless, multi-ethnic community of all God's people. Are there groups missing in our church community – who, why? Is everyone welcome? Then, we need to ask if our church leadership reflects the diversity of the membership.

Love in action

Jesus preached God's word but always had compassion for the suffering, healed the sick, included the outcast and loved the unloved. In Luke 17:11–19, Jesus had compassion on the lepers, excluded by society; he set them free from their state of exclusion and poverty through healing them. However, only the most socially excluded, the Samaritan, thanked Jesus, and Jesus commended his faith. Jesus exuded love, and the healed man found new faith in Jesus.

Demonstrating Jesus' love practically, being involved in social action and sharing the good news are not separate domains. As it has been said in Lausanne, they are two wings of a bird or two blades of a pair of scissors – one without the other has no use.[2]

In Acts 6, we saw how the neglected groups, victims of poverty, were cared for. A practical solution had to be found so that the apostles could get on with their task of proclaiming Jesus. The deacons were called to a vocation of practical service, but they also utilised their spiritual gifts as evangelists, notably Stephen and Philip. In fact, Philip had a heart for the marginalised, though his duties as deacon and through the people he met and preached to. As we prayerfully show Jesus' love in practical ways, through Christian projects, then we reflect Jesus and become his agents to allow others to encounter him.

I am increasingly aware that as projects grow, they rely on secular funding, set up separate trustees, and may employ non-Christian workers and accept non-church volunteers due to legislation. The founding intention of the project to reflect Jesus may be lost and the Christian identity and ethos may be diluted. This is something that all management trustees should be conscious of, and address. A regular, constant prayer life and partnership between church and project must be foundational and intentional. It is a constant challenge to uphold the project's integrity with its desire to be evangelistic.

Challenge: How can we show Jesus' love practically, desiring to reflect Jesus' love and expecting opportunities to share our faith? We may be involved in church ministry: preaching, worship, small group leader, Sunday school . . . the list goes on. But have we thought about how we can bring good news to the poor? Is there somewhere you can volunteer? Projects are often desperate for sound, Christian volunteers. What about being a trustee for a project if you have the gifts necessary? Is there a project you can pray for and raise awareness of? That would be a marvellous support and encouragement. Or could you support a food bank? Ultimately, the challenge is for each of us to look outwards more, to journey with God, as did Paul and the apostles. They were not afraid of going to unfamiliar places to spread the good news, see healing and witness new faith born. As in Acts 4, if they saw need, they responded. We often think that need is too far away to engage with, but it may be very close by.

The Victorian evangelical missionaries were often drawn to India and Africa, and saw these as alluring, yet widely overlooked the plight of those living in the UK's slums. I believe this view of mission as happening 'far away' has permeated the evangelicals. Noteworthy exceptions were Reverend William Pennefather and his wife, Catherine. From 1864, he was vicar of St Jude's, Mildmay, Islington, the church where I served as curate in more recent years. William and Catherine developed a number of social projects in a needy area, showing Jesus' love in action, whilst not erring from a desire to preach Christ crucified. These included soup kitchens, libraries, green spaces and home nursing. They set up a famous army of deaconesses to serve their community. In 1866, when there was a cholera outbreak in east London, two of the Mildmay deaconesses volunteered to go into some of London's worst slums to care for the sick. This became Mildmay Mission Hospital, which still exists, now caring for those with HIV. Pennefather is someone who has inspired me. He was unafraid of reaching out to the poorest and neediest, whilst having an evangelistic ministry.

Being prophetic

Being prophetic signifies that we are in tune with God, and seeking to listen out for his guidance. In Chapter 3, I observed that in many urban/estate contexts, through rapid decline the church is losing its prophetic edge, its *raison d'être* – to represent Jesus Christ and to be the focus of its community. As we are called to be missional (Matthew 28:19–20), we are required to grow the church of God. Through growing, both numerically and spiritually, we will have more strength and more resilience, more capacity to serve and to proclaim Christ. Growing God's kingdom is at the heart of all that occurs in Acts. Luke does not shy away from numbers (Acts 2:41; 6:7), nor should we. To grow physically, there is need to be healthy, and failing to diagnose disease will only lead to premature death.

Challenge: How healthy is your church? How outward-looking are you?

In Chapter 7, I said that Stephen the martyr was a prophet, annunciating God's voice to bring people back into a covenant relationship with him. Stephen spoke out in the mould of the Old Testament prophets, and I believe that many evangelicals and charismatics have been oblivious to this form of prophecy. Historically, there was the fear among evangelicals/charismatics of being tainted as liberal through engaging in social action. Fortunately, I think we have broken though this fear, and social action is back on the agenda. Significant evangelical prophets and reformers included William Wilberforce, Josephine Butler and William Booth, who campaigned and brought about major change in their time.

In our divided society, with much inequality and injustice, there remains the need to proclaim God's word into our society, pointing people back to God's measure of justice (Micah 6:8). In a climate of welfare reform, homelessness, increased poverty and xenophobic hostility, there is much campaigning to be done, much evil to be challenged and God's just ways to be proclaimed.

Challenge: What areas of injustice in your area can you practically help with? Are there isolated groups, such as asylum seekers, the elderly or single parents that your church can support? Is there community organising in your area that you could get involved with, working with others constructively to campaign on issues? Online there are many petitions and calls to contact your MP. Being salt and light (Matthew 5:13–16) means we should not be hiding our light under a bushel, but getting our hands dirty, though expressing God's displeasure at injustice and suffering.

Archbishop Desmond Tutu reminds us all that God calls us to be his agents of transformation in the part of the world we are set in: 'If God is transfiguring the world, you may ask, why does he need our help? The answer is quite simple: we are the agents of transformation that God uses to transfigure his world.'[3] He tirelessly lived this out, not losing hope but focusing on God and his vision for change.

My hope is that you have been inspired to look at the book of Acts with fresh eyes and have received a more focused understanding of the setting in which Luke wrote. Luke's passion was to see this young, fresh, energetic church grow, in the power of the Spirit, to see lives transformed, to witness the kingdom come through proclamation, healings and miracles. Significantly, Luke's vision of the kingdom of God breaking in to the world was a fervent desire to obliterate poverty, break down racism and social barriers. In short, God's church is for all God's people. It expresses the kingdom values of justice, mercy and acceptance. It should be a reflection of heaven, where God's rule has finally broken in. It should be a place where there is no more poverty, pain, suffering, inequality, where all races live together in peace, women and men, there are no marginalised people or groups, no hunger, sickness or depression.

A vision in Revelation describes how all human-made barriers will be broken down:

> After this I looked, and there before me was a great multitude that no one could count, from every nation, tribe, people and language, standing before the throne and before the Lamb. They were wearing white robes and were holding palm branches in their hands. And they cried out in a loud voice:
> 'Salvation belongs to our God,
> who sits on the throne,
> and to the Lamb' . . .
> 'Never again will they hunger;
> never again will they thirst.
> The sun will not beat down on them,'
> nor any scorching heat.
> For the Lamb at the centre of the throne
> will be their shepherd;
> 'he will lead them to springs of living water.'
> 'And God will wipe away every tear from their eyes.'
>
> Revelation 7:9–10; 16–17

In the present age, we are God's agents, his agents to herald in his kingdom, to bring about justice, to work towards wiping out those things that mar God's image in our society. The call is to be active now. In the book of Acts, the apostles and believers were open to the Holy Spirit leading them to break down barriers. They were radical in the way they shared all things and obeyed with excitement, venturing out to those on the edge.

But where do we begin? From my experiences in India, I concur with Mark Tully (BBC correspondent in India 1965–94) that there have been enough tears shed to fill the Ganges several thousand times, but I also learned that every small act of mercy makes a big difference. As Mother Teresa remarked: 'Not all of us can do great things. But we can do small things with great love.'[4] As Christians, may we be resolute in being God's agents of change, seeing his kingdom come in its fullest sense. May we be Holy Spirit Radicals.

Endnotes

1. www.theguardian.com/women-in-leadership/2014/may/01/ (accessed 1.5.14).
2. www.lausanne.org/content/covenant/lausanne-covenant (accessed 6.12.14).
3. Desmond Tutu, *God Has a Dream: A Vision of Hope for Our Time* (London: Rider, 2004), Kindle location 224.
4. www.goodreads.com/quotes/6946 (accessed 27.1.18).